DESTINATION:
FIERCE

*Moving from Fear
to Fierce*

CATHY JOY HILL

WESTBOW
PRESS®
A DIVISION OF THOMAS NELSON
& ZONDERVAN

WestBow Press books may be ordered through booksellers or by contacting:

WestBow Press
A Division of Thomas Nelson & Zondervan
1663 Liberty Drive
Bloomington, IN 47403
www.westbowpress.com
844-714-3454

Scripture quotations taken from The Holy Bible, New International Version® NIV®
Copyright © 1973 1978 1984 2011 by Biblica, Inc. TM. Used
by permission. All rights reserved worldwide.

ISBN: 978-1-6642-1394-4 (sc)
ISBN: 978-1-6642-1395-1 (hc)
ISBN: 978-1-6642-1393-7 (e)

Library of Congress Control Number: 2020923452

Print information available on the last page.

WestBow Press rev. date: 02/08/2021

Pour Dieu seul.

For God alone.

Contents

Acknowledgments

To my husband and my dream, Brian, as a little girl, God told me to wait for my knight in shining armor. Who knew he would be sitting in a foyer in Paris? Only God. I have loved you since that first day as a friend, then a husband, and finally my dearest companion throughout this life. You have pointed me to Jesus, and you point our children and so many others to the Savior. I am blessed beyond the greatest measure to walk with you. It has been a wild and wonderful ride. Thank you.

To my children, Bailey and Anya, Beau, Lily, and Ava Joy, if these words never go past your eyes alone, it will be worth it. More than anything, I want you to know Jesus as your Savior, best friend, closest confidant, and dearest companion. The greatest joy of my life, outside of marrying your daddy, has been mothering you. You are the essence of eternity to me, along with love, forgiveness, joy, and learning. Thank you.

To my brother Craig and his dear, sweet family, Karen, Nicholas, and Matthew, I have had the privilege not only to grow up with you but to grow old with you in business. Besides Daddy, you are the wisest man I know. You have inspired me and taken the business to places I never thought we would go, all while keeping true to God, your family, and what Mom and Daddy taught us, to be kind and loving in all circumstances. Thank you.

To Pastor Kurt, Jodi, and my second family, Amanda, Kristen, Brooke, and Micah, thank you for loving and leading. This life together has been a double blessing. To our beloved church, Sanctuary, thank you for letting me teach and lead in ways that are so undeserved yet have so blessed and grown me.

To Candy and Greg, thank you for the relentless encouragement. You are truly my adopted blessings.

To my cherished friends, I cannot count or name you all and do you the justice you deserve. You are my support, inspiration, and untold joy. Thank you.

To Lee and James Hill, Mom and Dad, and my sisters in love, Kim and Junell, you have raised my husband to be a fierce man of God. Thank you.

To my work family. We have sojourned so many years as so much more than coworkers. You have been a consistent source of joy and growth in my personal and professional life. I thank God for each of you.

Bienvenue Welcome

Let's imagine we are traveling together, you and I. Perhaps we know each other well; maybe we have just met. No matter, we are going to the same place, the land of Fierce.

We are going to learn a great deal together. We are going to sit with each other for the duration of this journey and walk and talk through each stop along the way. We may not know much about our destination, but with each stop and place we travel and traverse, we will look inside to explain what we see. Fierce is a destination. It is a place where we will arrive after we have forged the journey from fear.

We start at fear. I am not sure what your fear looks like—maybe disappointment, despair, failure, or feeling forsaken. But remember, we are not running from fear as much as we are walking away to find new places and ways of thinking. At each new place, six stops in all, we will read scripture, embrace prayer, and establish thought processes to keep us moving forward.

You and I have both packed light. We need each other and some scripture that I have already packed for us, and at each stop, we will pour some tea so we can relax and truly reflect on each new place we go, each new thought we have, and every way the Holy Spirit is allowing us to see new things.

He is marvelous this way. He wants this for us. It is not His will that any of us remain stuck in a place of fear; nor is it His will that we ever walk alone. He is our companion and counselor, and we ask Him to be part of this journey.

We begin at the beginning, with the word *fierce*. I like the ring of that word. I love the grit it suggests. I was attempting to put together a teaching for the lovely ladies in my church, and this word kept traveling through my mind. But it is not so much because of who I am. It is rather what I wanted. I knew a lot about fear; FIERCE was quite another story.

I wrote the word in all caps. My dad wrote every email he ever wrote in caps. When he said something, he meant it. I wanted to know what fierce meant. It felt and is the opposite of fear, but we cannot wish it into being. We must dissect it and experience every piece of it. That is the essence of this book, a step-by-step journey. I am so glad you are here with me.

I know a few things about the Holy Spirit:

1. He is an encourager.
2. He leads with the softest embrace. Opening a door to Him is the resurrection of hope. The despair and loneliness we have brought are exchanged for holy design and companionship.
3. He is wildly creative. He constantly astonishes me with the incredible reminders and reassurances of what He sees us (you and me) capable of doing with His help.
4. He comes to us and works through us to do extraordinary things we cannot possibly imagine doing in our strength or our own power. That is Him, all Him, filling the gaps of the creative grid He places in each of us.

More than anything, in picking up this book, I am praying with everything in me that it points you to the Holy Spirit, God our beloved Father, and Jesus Christ. Jesus Christ, God's Son, reconciles us through His death and resurrection on the cross.

I hope I can do Him some measure of justice in these words by recounting what He has done in my steps toward FIERCE-ness. I hope these words point you to His words and Him. Our salvation is without question the dearest gift we could ever receive, but alongside that and intrinsically and inescapably part of that salvation is His Word.

I have come to love His Word. I have come to relish every morning I can spend reading His Word. When we talk about fear, passion, or purpose in the coming pages, never forget the answers to all those things and everything is in scripture.

I will never forget when one of my dearest friends gave birth to her twins. Brian and I had been married just a few years and had begun serving with her and her pastor husband. It was very early in her pregnancy. We had just finished Wednesday service when I heard her crying, a heartbreaking sob, in the basement of our church. I ran downstairs with Brian and her husband. She said three words, "I am bleeding." And with that, her husband whisked her off to the emergency room.

Brian and I went home and prayed. Ultimately the hospital saw fit to send her home. She was still carrying what we thought was one baby, and even with this bit of bleeding, all seemed well.

They lived just far enough from the church that we agreed she should come to my house, which was much closer to the hospital. I made her tea and sat by her bedside. To this day, I recall those moments. A breaking heart needs someone to hold its pieces. I was one of the holders that night, and we have been glued together ever since. I read Psalm 91 and prayed.

She is younger than I am, but even in those early days, she had a vast knowledge of scripture that I envied. When I met her mom and daddy, I could see they had fostered a love of scripture and scriptural center in their home life that was truly beautiful. I held her parents, who are both now in heaven, in the very highest esteem. When either of them spoke, recommended a book, or prayed, I stopped and listened.

Some months after that Wednesday night, roughly eight months later, she sat at that same hospital holding the most precious two babies I had ever seen. Her daddy spoke these incredible words, "You will only ever need one set of instructions, and you can find them all in the Bible. The Bible has everything you will ever need to know about how to parent these children and absolutely everything else." He was so right.

My dear friend had her babies in September. That December we learned we were pregnant with our first son. I earnestly started reading the Word then, devotions at first and then scripture. In all the confusion of the world, the Word is the one true, unfailing constant. It is living and breathing. It edifies, encourages, directs, and helps us discern. It narrates the lives of people just like you and me, the flawed and failing who learned through the Holy Spirit to be fierce.

Dear one, perhaps just the thought of scripture—reading and studying it—is daunting at best. I am there with you. My children, husband, brother, and friends will attest that I am no scholar, and the first minutes, or perhaps years, of reading my Bible were halted and hard. We will get to that, believe me.

Please don't close this book just yet. Hang in and hang on. I cannot make it easier, but I know without a shadow of a doubt that the Holy Spirit can. He is in this work. He tells us clearly, "For God gave us a spirit not of fear but of power and love and self-control" (2 Timothy 1:7 ESV).

That power, the power to become fierce, is where we begin.

Fierce

So what is fierce? Anytime I have learned anything, such as a foreign language or business principle, I have had to take it in bits. God knows this about me. I have big ideas, but I have to start with very little steps. How do you eat an elephant? The answer is "one bite at a time."

The very word *fierce* suggests power, specifically a positive or intense power. Fierce, as the dictionary defines, is "showing a heartfelt and powerful intensity." And it gives this example, "He kissed her with a fierce passion." It is the following:

- The idea of a love shared and exchanged
- The idea of someone pursuing us with passion
- The idea that someone loves you and demonstrates that love for you in an extraordinary and demonstrative way

Our Father possesses an incredible passion for His children. He is crazy in love with us.

Fear likewise is powerful. It can encumber, encase, and immobilize the warrior, saint, athlete, and us. We have all felt it. We all feel it. We stand at the garden with Eve and wonder what we will miss if … Her fear of not knowing something God knew enticed her to the fruit. She and Adam's fear of their nakedness forged the first clothes. Their fear of God's wrath wrote their first lie. Fear is where we are starting. Fierce is where we want to go.

Let's look around for just a moment. Look outside with me. What do you see? Is it blue skies or gentle rain? Is it a dazzling sunset or zinnias blooming in the yard? Is it fall leaves or freshly fallen snow? We do not have to look far to find Him. He sees us and says, "Just so you know, I am here. I am going to paint a different sunrise and sunset each and every single day."

He gives us plain old dirt for nine months out of the year, but come April, May, and June, watch out. Flowers will take over. The peonies will blossom in May; the zinnias will follow in July. He grows any seed we choose to plant so long as we allow them to see sun and deliver water. He is everywhere in every month. In September and October, we harvest the apples, pumpkins, and gourds with every shape and warm, beautiful color known to man—oops— God. In the winter, the snow flies, and we are reminded of His creativity. Every flake is a different design, like us, you and me.

There are no two of us with completely matching DNA. You and I may be structurally the same, but some part of our DNA, written distinctly different, makes you and I unique from one another. As every person will testify, no matter how many children they have, adopt, or love, not one of their babies will turn out the exact same.

We all have a significant part in the natural and supernatural kingdom of God. He wastes nothing, and not one person on this planet is here without purpose. He puts different prints on our fingers, passions in our hearts, and skills in our hands and minds. He arranges divine appointments throughout our lives to bring us to people and places we need to mix the ingredients for our delicious purpose.

He allows suffering, the actual root of the word *passion* (Merriam-Webster). From fear to fierce and passion from suffering, the two have a taut tension. One is so welcome; the other is, yes, feared. I had you there until that sentence, yes?

Not one person enjoys suffering, yet the apostle John warns us, "In this world, we will have trouble" (John 16:33). He was not kidding. And our trouble, as daunting as it may be, is different, mine from yours and everyone else. We might share our burdens, yet only He knows the depth and breadth of our heartache. Only He knows how long it will last. Only He knows our time in the desert. Only He understands how long the wait in the hospital or longing for our prodigal son will be. Only He is sure when and if the hurt will go away. In this space, this suffering space, passion is often born.

I adored my mother with every square inch of my being. Her years of suffering with bipolar disorder were absolutely the worst years of my life. But that terrible time has given me a wild heart of compassion for those who suffer with mental illness. I want them to see there is no stigma. I want us to love the mentally ill exactly as Jesus loves His church. I want to include them in our parties and planning. I want them to know that their illness is our illness and our church is part of their hospital.

We all suffer at some time in some space and for a most definite reason. God does not waste suffering. Instead He allows it. And as much as I hate to admit it, the times I have known and loved Him best was when I have hurt the worst. In those horribly long, dark seasons, He was the only thing in my heart that had not broken, and He was the only thing I could rely upon through long days and impossibly hard nights.

As a mama, we shudder at the thought of our children hurting. Two of mine have had multiple surgeries. When my youngest son was four and my baby girl was eight, it was different circumstances, hospitals, ages, doctors, and recoveries. I saw these two children cry out to Jesus, not because I told them to but because that was what their heart longed for. Their faith is different because of these times. I cannot say it is bigger or better than their other two siblings. It is simply different. It was born out of suffering; perhaps yours is too.

Fierce is part bringing Jesus closer, part knowing your passion, and part fleeing from fear. When this word wandered into my heart, the six pieces built this acronym, and for us, it is our map, our itinerary. These are the places we will stop and stay for a bit. Some you will know very well; others may be new. Stay with me, dear one. By the grace of the Holy Spirit, we will learn together.

F—Foundation - knowing who we are in Christ
I—Inviting Jesus into every corner of our lives
E—Experiencing His presence
R—Rejoice - embracing joy at all times in all circumstances
C—Calling - what He has made us for
E—Enlarging our territory
How do we move from fear to fierce? I am so glad you asked.

2

Fear and Some Fake Fans

We are boarding our train at fear. We want to remember where we have been and why God has allowed this place. The Hill House dictionary defines *fake fan* as someone who jumps on the popular bandwagon at the last moment when it becomes the vogue, fashionable thing to do.

I have an environmentalist living in my house. If one of their siblings opts for a metal straw in our solidarity "to save turtles," they too are branded a "fake fan." As strange as it is, I have come to grips with the fact that I am a fake fan of fear. It's weird, I know, but bear with me.

I have long read and learned in the church that fear is bad. If you think about fear, the phrase "do not fear" immediately pops into mind. I have heard preachers say, "Do not fear appears in the Bible 365 times," a reminder that every day, 365 times each year, we better not be afraid. But let's take a good, long look at fear. Perhaps it is not always the fiend we have given it credit for.

We raise our children with some element of natural fear. I wanted my toddlers to be afraid to cross a street, run through a parking lot, or put their fingers on a hot stove. I wanted them to be afraid with the knowledge that disobedience could be incredibly detrimental. We embrace our children with knowledge in the portions they can understand.

When we had three children, we took a sentimental journey back to France. My husband, Brian, and I met there as students, and we were determined to show our history to our babies. We took them to our school and the beautiful Jardin du Luxembourg. Our two youngest were four and six. The practicality of this was not our strong suit, but we were passionate to show them Paris. They are wonderful travelers and endured miles of walking. They were rewarded with chocolate crepes wherever we could find them. All was well until we ventured down to the metro.

We were waiting for the train, as we had done hundreds of times as students, when our youngest son decided to take a look at the subterranean track. I didn't see him, but my husband did. At the moment our son, Beau, was just about to peek over the walkway downward, Brian saw that the metro was fast approaching. Brian reached out and grabbed our six-year-old by the hair. It was not eloquent, but it was effective. I remember tearing up at what might have been.

This is what fear, the biochemical kind, does. It prompts us to action and reaction. It does not think; it acts. It is responsible for the immediate call to 9-1-1. It prompts everyday people to save lives, fight fires, and defend the helpless. It is good and it is energizing. It can prevent very bad things from happening. It is the fight-or-flight reaction, as Walter Cannon coined. We move based on our hearts first ("Walter Cannon: Stress & Fight or Flight Theories").

As my children have gotten older, I have relied on the same sense of fear. I have told them that no good things happen after midnight. I mention countless times that our life is the sum total of all of our decisions. I have prayed that they would make wise choices with friends and to choose wisely what they invite into their minds as they peruse the internet or entertainment. I want them to fear the consequences. I know I do.

Many souls have been saved through fear. I had a conversation with my eldest son on the phone. He spent four wonderful years at an amazing Christian college just thirty minutes away from home. As I write, he is attending graduate school at a secular university nine hours away. To both of us, the culture shock has been huge.

Every week I ask him where he went to church or how the preaching was. At twenty-three years old, he is an adult, but us mamas never stop being mamas. He mentioned to me that there is a street-side preacher on his campus of 45,000 students. The preacher yells to those walking by, "Are you forgiven?" and "Do you know Jesus?"

I have to admit this brought a smile to my face. I love that kind of moxie, and I already love this preacher. My son, however, said the most interesting thing. "Millennials do not like a gospel of fear."

I found this fascinating. I do not for one minute debate the veracity of this statement, but isn't fear a part of the gospel?

I will get to the fear of the Lord in a minute, which quite frankly is not a biochemical fear. Rather the thought of hell scares the pudding out of me. I do not want to live without the presence of the Holy Spirit. I do not want to be in a lake of fire. I cannot imagine being separated from my heavenly Father. Although I appreciate my son's thoughts tremendously, I have been to more than one camp meeting where I found myself at the altar just to be sure my sins were not taking me to hell.

Fear, my beloved, can be good. Perhaps discerning where our fear is coming from and what it has taught us is worth our time. Perhaps we can be a fan, fake or not, of the fear that has kept us physically safe and the fear that first led us to Jesus.

The devil authors the paralyzing, irrational kind of fear, which is the type we need to fear. That fear is not of God, yet He absolutely knows it is real and tempting and keeps us from Him. It is an overarching barrier to the love and peace of Christ. It takes a million forms and speaks a million languages. It says phrases like, "What will people think?" and "And if only then." It also accuses. It says lies like, "You are stupid," "No one likes you," "You are ugly," or "You don't have what it will take." And like so much of what the devil slips into our ears, it is oh so subtle. Fear comes in dozens of forms. The devil does not discriminate by ethnicity, age, or gender. He is a pro at fearmongering.

Let's talk about the devil for just a moment. The devil is not the Creator. He does not create. He cannot inhabit our minds, but he can and does whisper in our ears. His tool is often fear, which plays multiple parts in our role as God's children. Perhaps you know them: worry, self-doubt, self-hatred, jealousy, paranoia, control, perfectionism, and hatred. It is the whisper of something you would never hope for your best friend or your dearest love, yet you entertain these thoughts. God says the same thing you would say to your friend who begins to believe the lie. "Stop! Do not believe the lie. You are so much more than this. You are God's amazing creation made in His image by His hand to do the extraordinary things He has called you to do." Believe this.

I once heard a preacher say, "If your mind has a thought that you would not wish for itself, perhaps it is authored by the enemy." When we moved back home to my hometown near Chicago, Brian had transferred, and I had to find a job. Every day I would send résumés and make calls. All this occurred in my dad's little office. He had retired but was puttering about in a new company to keep busy.

I was intrigued with his ingenuity, but the idea of a steady paycheck seemed far sturdier than a start-up. Finally the offer came, a new job in the heart of Chicago, using my second language and traveling the world. Brian and I were thrilled. Thoughts of helping Dad with his start-up vanished.

A few weeks later, I was packed and ready for training in New York when a call came that I had not passed the company physical. I had a growth on my thyroid. This was clearly a deal-breaker.

My mom had endured thyroid cancer. I knew this was nothing to trifle with. The job was now gone. Weeks later, the doctor confirmed mine was benign. I needed surgery, but I also needed a job. Brian and I sat down. Brian was convinced the work I was doing with my dad was the footprint for a successful company. I did not want to own my own company. The risk seemed to suffocate me. The fear of failure felt like burial before birth. But we had nothing else—no other offers and no other prospects.

The passport to fear is stamped with words like "if only" and "if you were or would have been." The passage out of fear, the one that leads to freedom, is solely of God. "So if the Son sets you free, you are free indeed" (John 8:36). And know that He has never created someone and wanted a redo. .

We look at our children as beautiful. Their eyes, faces, hair, personalities, quirks, and gifts are all unique and part of a divine masterpiece to bring Him glory. Why do we not see ourselves the same way?

I am crazy in love with art, especially the French masters. Yet I have trouble drawing a decipherable stick figure. My husband is an incredible singer. Some of my best friends sing so beautifully that their worship or Broadway songs can bring me to joyful tears, yet I can barely hold a note. I have occasionally thought that He missed something.

We are terrible at seeing ourselves as He sees us. He observes us as His creation, His chef-d'oeuvre. "For we are God's workmanship, created in Christ Jesus to do good works, which God prepared in advance for us to do" (Ephesians 2:10). We are His workmanship. In many translations, we are His masterpiece. Dear heart, we are hanging in his Louvre for people to look at and say, "Only a true Master could have created that."

Perhaps you are struggling with your gifting, your calling. We will get there, I promise. I just want to make sure if you feel you do not have a gift or if you feel you are not good, not His, or not worthy, I promise you with every last inch of me, it is our mutual enemy, the devil, trying to convince you of this lie. Our God does not make mistakes. He is always good, and He wastes absolutely nothing.

I have found the devil is strategic. For me, it is typically a three-pronged attack and not in any specific order. He goes after me personally—my self-esteem, my intelligence, my skills, or lack thereof. Second, he targets my work, creativity, church, or home. He has no flavor of the day. Then he looks to my family, my husband, or my kids. I will come home from a failed bid or a difficult meeting and find that I have forgotten to get the tux dry-cleaned for the concert or the poster board purchased for the project.

Little things, when tied together, produce words like disappointment and failure. Perhaps you hear these words like I do. Possibly you hear adjectives like stupid, ugly, fat, or failure. Maybe you believe these terms. Perhaps you have defined yourself this way. Possibly like I did for so many years and still occasionally do, I define myself by what I do, not what He did, or I focus on my accomplishments, not His redemption.

We are made in the image of Christ. We are the very reflectors of Him, and that changes everything. If we allow the devil to define us, he and we build a prison. We measure our steps, calling, and "busyness" based on the lies we believe.

Yet as much as I am aware of how he works, so often the actual attack is out of left field. We must have spiritual eyes. We must ask the Holy Spirit daily to allow us to see with His eyes. Irritatingly our enemies can feel like people, situations, or randomness. We can blame the devil for absolutely everything wrong or far too little.

I have played into the devil's hands many times, getting irritated with people and not praying. I have also allowed things like unforgiveness to well up in me and blamed the devil for my own lack of obedience. We hurt, and like a wounded child, we nurse our hurt and target the person(s) who dealt the blow. Spiritual eyes? I might need bifocals.

Last night, I returned home from a business trip, a one-day meeting. I got up this morning and threw my work clothes into the washer. It occurred to me that I spent probably thirty minutes figuring out what I was going to wear to those meetings. It matters, yes, that we are professional, but truly, thirty minutes? It's a little much. And yet I think little or nothing about my preparedness for the daily agenda of spiritual battles. I do read scripture. I love it, but I rarely think of it as preparedness for battle. To win battles, we must have a strategy. Paul tells us in Ephesians what our attire is. Isn't it fun to think our wardrobe is picked out? We just found ourselves thirty minutes.

Have Ephesians 6 dog-eared in your Bible. Read it as a treatise and trust. Go through the attire like your life depends on it because it does. Buckle in truth, cover your heart with the knowledge that you are saved by grace and right with Jesus, and shadow your feet with the Word. Have scripture ready, and if you cannot think of one, Jesus's name will dispel the enemy from your mind. Some of us hold on to praise choruses; others cling to His name. A few have 2 Timothy 1:7 woven in, "He does not give us a spirit of fear, but of power, love and a SOUND MIND" (emphasis added).

On my very first business trip over twenty-five years ago, I had an international flight. I was still extremely overwhelmed that we had started a company and felt I needed to learn things like time management. I picked up Steven Covey's book, *Seven Habits of Highly Effective People*. To this day, some 1,300 weeks after I have read that text, I use one simple principle that I learned. I list out the roles I play, roughly six or seven, and next to them I write what each role will require of me that week.

These are the roles you play as well: wife or husband, mother or father, teacher, sister, friend, employee, volunteer, and so forth. I am a wife, mother, business owner, women's ministry leader, friend, and sister. I have learned the hard way that if one of these roles has two or three responsibilities next to it, I need to find a way to ease the burden on the other five or six roles. This means the family may need to pitch in or we may have fast food for dinner (more than once in a week). It could mean I have to cancel an appointment or find someone to cover a school obligation. It always means I have to pray hard.

For years, one of the roles I wrote was "child of God." I did not list it as a role as much as a reminder I needed to start my day with Him.

For years I found that morning quiet time, as we deem it in the church, enough, but then two years ago, as I write these words, almost to this very day, my daddy died.

My dad lived an extraordinary life. He was born a child of the Great Depression. He would tell stories of his daddy not having a nickel to send him to the fair and how his daddy cried that day. That story still breaks me, the sorrow of his sweet daddy, my granddaddy, and the charter it gave my dad and his brothers. They became some of the hardest working, most intelligent men I have ever had the fortune to know.

Some, including Daddy, went to war. He thought it was the right thing to do, but it was also his ticket to higher education, and educated he became. He took care of an old doctor for room and board while he studied to become an engineer. He had the greatest sense of humor of anyone I have ever known. He was a self-made man who had a successful career and then came into the company my brother and I formed for twenty-five years, never once asking for anything but coffee and a bit of desk space. We made thousands of trips to McDonald's for coffee and talked about the day's agenda or issues. He was a gift to me as a dad and a precious grandfather to my and my brother's children.

He told me on Easter Sunday he was not feeling well. Three weeks later as my brother and I slept next to him, he met Jesus. I could not fathom the hole his leaving would carve. We had lost mom twelve years earlier. She was the sweetest, gentlest woman. But when Daddy left, I felt the crushing weight of having no parents to share life with, no confidant in the office, and no grandpa nearby to watch over my children.

For days I could not stand the sight of his empty desk. For months I wondered when the pain of loss would lessen. I began to take God with me to work. He became more than something on my weekly list. He was faithful as I cried and so willing to listen to the questions I would have asked Daddy. I feared with everything in me I could not run the company without him. The suffering has transformed me. James 4:8 tell us that as we "draw near to Him, He will draw near to us." He does.

In this crazy, mixed-up, demanding, busy, be-everything-to-everyone life, we must remember His place. He is not on the list; He owns the list. Our ability to do, be, and succeed is all Him. Our skills, passions, people, houses, cars, work, and stuff are His. The conversations we have, the places we go, and the things we do, all of it and everything is part of the piece we hold in His kingdom and for His glory. The idea that He wants us to run, chase, perform, and be weary and worn out and do it all again the next day is nothing short of insanity and a big fat, demonic lie. The devil is the author of lies. It has taken me so long to learn that weary is not worship.

Jesus is the one person who saw heaven before He came to earth. His list of six or seven roles and His execution of His responsibilities is worth a long look. He walked, ate, and spent quality, unrushed time with those He met. I don't sense He rushed. His actions always had the added weight of eternity. So do ours. He was the very definition of hospitality, to welcome and walk, that is, not jog and judge.

He saw the end quite literally from the beginning. We have the travel brochure. As redeemed believers, we see it as well. It is this fear of the Lord where we depart, where we leave unhealthy, unholy lives and hold hands with Him.

Look at those words, the "fear of the Lord." After all we have said, thought, and feared fear, are these words from Proverbs? I have long thought of them as a little daunting. We do not serve a capricious God or a God that offers us blessings but makes them unattainable. He tells us repeatedly to not fear. Then why is there the "fear of the Lord"?

I think it is extraordinary that in the English language, this word inhabits both our disdain and admiration. Fear is both biochemical and demonic, and in this sense, it is the awe-inspiring hope of someone who is bigger and better than both.

A few nights ago, I was flying into Chicago. I have flown this route dozens of times. It is spring so the days are longer, and my typical night flight ended in sunset instead of darkness. I had left a particularly hard meeting. We are making decisions as a company I never thought we would face. The weight of them pressed on my chest. I inhaled a book as we traveled home, disappointed to arrive at the last page before the runway.

I looked out of my window seat. We were still a few hundred miles out, but as far as I could see, a burning orange glow surrounded absolutely everywhere I looked. It held the land and lake as far as I could see. It was like a burning hot shell over every inch of everything, hanging just above the surface. Perhaps it was the angle, but I have never seen a sunset so magnificent.

I was flying alone. My thoughts were my own. The problems and possibilities weighed, but looking out that window, it was as if God were holding the earth with an orange ribbon tied tightly around every corner. With every nuance of the land, not one inch escaped Him. "The fear of the Lord is the beginning of wisdom" (Proverbs 9:10).

Fear, awe, respect, admiration, and the take-your-breath-away idea that He is holding the entire planet in this fiery, orange strip of light shows me He is here. He is in control, and nothing—not one moment, thought, or doubt—has escaped Him. It was as if He looked down and said, "Let me show you how big, wide, and great my love is."

I felt Him there all around, in, and through me. I don't know how this will go, but I do know how it will end. I am absolutely convinced we, or me, have forgotten to fear Him. God is Judge, King, and Father. The camp meeting hellfire-and-brimstone preacher is partial to the Judge. For years I have been so focused on the Father that I have forgotten the King.

The twenty-first-century church has focused on the Father, the loving, kind Father, and He is that and will always be. But He is also our Judge, our white-throned, Book of Life judge. Last, but certainly not least, He is King.

He is King of Kings and Lord of Lords, with all the power and authority the King of the Universe should command. He tossed both heaven and earth into existence. He breathed the breath into us, you and me, His Holy Spirit's breath with which we all exhale. He looks at you and me and says, "Dip into this power and let's do something together." Dear one, He does not need us. He wants us! The Master, the Creator, the Comforter, and the Counselor pursues us because he wants to!

It leaves me awestruck. But perhaps in a moment of fear—fear of failure or opinion—or moment when we are too busy to think of anything, much less Him, maybe we take the amazing out of grace and the miraculous out of mercy. Possibly our fear has not met the fear. The extraordinary gift of true fear of the Lord is bundled in trust and sealed with grace.

My daddy could have written a book on living and dying well. He had a Southern charm, a deep faith, a gut-busting humor, and wisdom. He earned his wisdom. He would always talk to my brother and me with more respect and admiration than we deserved. His words were few but measured and meaningful. As a little girl in scrapes with a friend and in business when I struggled to discern a client's needs or an employee's wants, Daddy would say, "Your perspective is only your perspective."

He would challenge me to see things from the other side of the playground, desk, or aisle. We are framed by our raising, experience, education, and emotions. We look out from our framing, and the world looks at ours. We meet somewhere in the middle, but only if we respect and acknowledge that our perspectives are and should be different.

When Daddy died, much of my perspective changed. Perhaps the framing of fear and our perspective of it requires the same sort of shift. Maybe we cannot escape the wiles of the devil, but we certainly can cozy them up and watch them obey the Word of God. "He who fears the Lord has a secure fortress, and for his children it will be a refuge. The fear of the Lord is the fountain of life, turning a man from the snares of death" (Proverbs 14:26).

We look again, and the fear we know and the faith we have moves the Father in front of the fear we dread. On this side of heaven, we will not dismiss fear. The devil makes sure of this, but tuning into godly fear rings loud. The fear of the Lord brings a mighty general to the battlefield. It reminds us that we are not alone and fierce is fought for with Him, not by Him. It allows us to split our anxiety with the axe of truth, and the parts that remain, that is, the worries and anxiety, are smaller because He holds them all.

3

Foundation

Our First Stop

I was raised in the church. I was one of those kids who began attending at two weeks old and never left. There were seasons when my parents were caring for their ailing parents and could not attend, but my brother and I were dropped off.

I learned faithfulness from that. I learned there was something good in those four walls, something I wanted to hang on to. The Holy Spirit is wonderfully good at setting things apart. The holiness of scripture, the truth of the Word, the mercy of Christ, and the grace of God are set apart in our hearts. We know they are true in the uncanny way the Holy Spirit confirms they are. He can handle our questions and doubts because the sacredness of it all will always be there. I felt it then; I know it now.

I am forever grateful that the church was a priority for my parents. I didn't always love it. I didn't always remember the sermons, and I wasn't able to recite the Bible verses, but the idea of building on a rock has always meant something. Not only is sand difficult to build on, it is difficult to navigate through. But it is not so with the gospel. The gospel is the same yesterday, today, and forever. It remains constant, strong, and true. It is absolutely something on which we can build our lives, and it never disappoints.

Perhaps you didn't go to church as a child; maybe you made the acquaintance later in life. Whatever brought you here, I am so grateful. You see, there is no better believer. There is no ranking in the body of Christ. Jesus made it clear that our faith goal should be the faith of a child, not by age, mind you, but the wide-eyed, full-of-wonder, the could-He-really-be-this-good kind of faith.

I hope that is where you are beginning. The recipe for a fierce life is a dash of wonder and a heaping portion of hungry faith. Faith causes our eyes to see, our ears to hear, and our hearts to yearn for more.

Faith has to start somewhere. As children, it is blind. It is the confidence in the birth, the absolute of the death and resurrection, and the fascination with lions that don't consume and fires that don't burn. It is allowing the living Word to do what living things do, breathe. The Word has to breathe into us to give us the ability to grow.

My son Beau was just eighteen months old, and we were in the full-fledged process of adopting our first daughter. We moved seven-tenths of a mile away from our starter home to add a bedroom and more living space. It was January and a blistering cold day. Because I am nothing if not frugal, we filled our cars and a truck and begged every friend at church to scale up our icy driveway and help us move in. I love my church. I love the way our peeps will lay down their agenda to help us or hold us up.

One of our dearest friends, Ron Kless, had come days before our closing and packed our garage. I don't know what it was about that garage, but neither Brian nor I could get it packed. It was too random, too much, and too unimportant compared to the five million things inside the house. He packed, pitched, and had us laughing the entire time. Whenever I think of Ron, I think of Him talking to Jesus. I also think of how suddenly his health turned and all of us were standing around his bed in the hospital. I recall how my son Bailey drew him a picture to take to the hospital that said, "You are the lucky one." Bailey knew Ron would soon meet Jesus. Facing big, like moving and mundane, I rarely consider myself lucky. But aren't we?

We moved in. Even stacked with boxes, it seemed empty. I knew it was 100 percent right, but even right can feel misplaced and hard when we try to do it all ourselves. My dearest baby son Beau went from easy and sweet to feisty and fussy. With the mayhem of moving, I put up with it for days until finally Brian and I decided we needed to call the pediatrician. I handed him to our pediatrician with two words, "fix him." Our trusted, sweet doctor checked every inch of him and could find absolutely nothing wrong.

I asked him to look at his ears one more time. Shaking his head, the doc asked if anything else had changed. I mentioned the move and tried to think if I had changed food or detergents. The doctor looked me straight in the eye and said, "Bingo!" He went on to explain that eighteen months was probably one of the worst ages to move a child. Beau could not verbalize his confusion or adjustment but knew he did not like it. Who knew?

I bundled up Beau. We went home and sat in our big, stuffed, red chair in our family room and cried. I missed our old house. I missed the memories of my mom taking care of our oldest son in that house. I missed the familiar.

Mom had gone home to see her Jesus. I had told her as she lay dying, we would be moving houses and adopting our little girl. I had told her we would be naming our daughter Lily in her honor. But she wasn't there to hold my hand and tell me it would all work out, we would love this house, and the memories that would be new would not take place of the old but add to them.

I looked outside. Our new house had a pond in the backyard. In the dusk of winter, ice sparkled off the water. I turned Beau around to look at it with me. I told him, "We are going to love this place."

Spring finally came, and the winter snow relented. We donned boots and spring jackets, and the boys and I headed to the pond. The ground was soft from the snow melting, but the frogs were already waking to spring, and the fish and bugs were coming to life. We got closer to the edge, trying to spot fish and tadpoles. Beau was in the middle, flanked by my seven-year-old Bailey and myself. He seemed no closer than we were, but in an instant, his little feet slipped into the water, and he began to sink fast.

It is a golf course pond, dug by man with what we learned a surprising depth and steep shore. Bailey and I each grabbed an arm and took our frightened baby out of the water, covered in mud from the chest down.

We learned something that day. The pond, the little golf course pond so full of life and wonder, was dangerous, and the Hill children would not be going anywhere close to it again. I also learned as the months and years passed that my rule did not apply to the neighbor children. Summer after summer, I watched as the neighbor kids walked near the pond and skipped rocks across it. Winter after winter, I saw my neighbor clear the snow and ice-skate with his children. I heard them roar with laughter as they played hockey and threw snowballs. All the while I watched, literally waiting to call 9-1-1. I had decided the pond was not safe, and I was sticking to it.

This last winter was exceptionally cold. I think in three months, we had 595 days of below-freezing temperatures. One Saturday, the air, although freezing, was bearable, and I watched as the neighbor kids played hockey. My daughter Ava Joy begged to join, but I redirected her to building a snowman. My husband gallantly bundled up to help, and I promised to come out and snap a picture. I was honestly grateful the hockey game had ended. There would be no discussion of hockey or ice skating. After a bit of snowman building, we would call it a day.

I saw Frosty go up and arrived with my camera and a carrot for the nose. I took the picture. I wasn't thinking about the pond but rather just took a bit of a walk. The snow was good packing snow, not the soft stuff that exhausts you after ten feet of walking. I made it all the way back to the pond.

It was solid. I realized it had been solid now for a very long time. We had not had a day above thirty-two degrees in what felt like years. There was absolutely no question: one could walk, slide, or skate across without any danger.

And I wondered what I had been missing. For almost fifteen years, I had banished my children from the pond because of fear. I wanted to step out on that pond, just one foot to say I could, to know that at least today fear would not get in the way. The water was solid, much like a life built on Jesus.

Where are you today? Are you like me, standing on the side of life, hoping you can muster the courage to walk out, take His hand, and experience the life He has promised? It will be hard, but remember, easy is not the goal. Glory is.

Maybe you are already out there. You have heard your call, but even the most solid of ice can be slippery. You have to grab His hand and keep holding. You dig into scripture and pray hard, but maybe the results or rewards aren't coming as fast as you thought. Perhaps it is lonely in the middle holding on to Him. Possibly the family has not understood or the friends have faded away. I get it. I have been there too.

And then some have made it. They have gone across the first big stretch of ice and are looking for the next. They are waving back at us and cheering us on because they know He is faithful. I am so glad you are here with us to encourage us. You whisper words of hope to us and we to you.

I am not sure when I fell in love with scripture. It was some years ago. It was not because of its eloquence; it was and is the contagion of knowing more about Jesus. Every day was a new journey; every passage was a new piece of this Jesus with whom I was falling deeper in love with. You have your path. Perhaps you have come out of pain or loss. Possibly you are giving Jesus your first try or you are on your very last nerve.

I will tell you until I am blue about scripture. I love it. I wake up for it. I am constantly and absolutely amazed about how I can read and then hear the same words in a story or song sometime later in my day or week. This is how the Holy Spirit works.

He is incredibly personal, deeply detailed, and wonderfully winsome. He weaves into our very souls the threads of lessons and love. This doesn't happen every single day, but when it does, it can only be explained by Him. I have filled up on a Sunday morning just to have an opportunity to pour out into the next day, evening, or week. He is crazy good this way, and I love Him for it.

He allows us to be children. Children need a parent, love, repetition, honesty, and trustworthiness that never disappoints or abandons and is never unavailable. Children need truth. They need a foundation.

Before I was so sentimental about scripture, I had a love affair with at least a dozen Christian authors. We are in an age and time where great, wise people are writing great, wise books. They are blogging, podcasting, and pouring out truth at a rate never before seen. And our venues for ministry, teaching, and learning are like nothing that has before existed.

Yes, some have lost their way and blurred truth, but we have multi-generations that are planting good seeds. The new generations are watering, and the sweet Spirit is harvesting as only He can.

I was reading one of these authors. One who uses scripture like a flame to ignite. I became passionate about Christine Caine, about her call to serve and her knowledge of scripture. I loved the way I felt watching videos of her teaching. I began to love her work, and I became so anxious to share her teachings with my church. I booked a plane ticket to see her in person. I wanted to be in her classroom and to share the presence of God in the same space.

I am profoundly blessed in a couple thousand ways to be married to the man I married, but number 642 in the blessings department is that he used to be in the travel business. I can casually mention a city, and he is shopping fares.

The city was Houston, which as I am sure you know is not terribly far from Waco, Texas. We are more than a little in love with the whole mojo of Magnolia. Within a matter of hours, Brian booked a flight to Dallas, a road trip to *Fixer Upper* heaven and then a straight shot to the holy of Houston. I was over the moon.

I am not sure I can actually define the timing as divine, but this all fell just days after my birthday, so in every way, at least to me, it felt like a birthday trip. My birthday also happens to be in November, so close to Christmas that I had two huge reasons to get serious about Texas treasure.

Our little girls, Brian, and I lined up at the Bakery at 7:00 a.m. It opens at 7:30 a.m., by the way, but there was absolutely nothing getting in the way of our Magnolia experience. We dined and drank the entire day as if savoring sweet tea. We went from department to department, imagining our home "fixed up" or at least freshened with a few new things.

I have never been a big shopper, perhaps not even a little one, but there was something beautiful about this place: the gardens and the food and seeing the real-life fulfillment of someone else's dream and success. I loved it. I felt like I had not just walked into a shop but the life of those that had achieved their dreams. We drank it in.

We left Magnolia late in the afternoon, bound for Houston and a short night before a long day of teaching. I was as excited about what I was going to hear and what I had just seen. I had my Bible, pencil, coffee, and notebook. I sat down close to the front and popped up as the worship music started. After months of waiting, the speaker came to the stage and began with, "Turn your Bibles to Psalm 23."

> The LORD is my shepherd, I shall not want. He makes me lie down in green pastures, he leads me beside still waters, he restores my soul. He leads me in the paths of righteousness for His name's sake. Yea though I walk

through the valley of the shadow of death, I will fear no evil, for you are with me; your rod and your staff, they comfort me. You prepare a table before me in the presence of my enemies. You anoint my head with oil; my cup runs over. Surely goodness and mercy will follow me all the days of my life, and I will dwell in the house of the LORD forever. (NKJV)

Psalm 23? I had grown up on this psalm. Hasn't every Christian who has ever lived or, for that matter, died known this psalm from beginning to end? I would say if we were asked to picture Christ, many of us would see him as the Shepherd that graced our Sunday school walls or children's Bible, the Psalm 23 Shepherd. I had this very psalm read in two languages at my wedding. To say I felt "I had been there and done that" would be no exaggeration. I didn't bother to open my Bible. I didn't have to.

The speaker didn't read the whole psalm. She started and finished with the first verse, in truth, the last four words. After nine words total, she hovered around the last four, "I shall not want" (Psalm 23:1b).

She asked me and the thousand or so people in the room to say it over and over again. To be honest, it was just a little irritating. But I am convinced she knew, or perhaps it was the Holy Spirit that I do wanting pretty well.

I don't want for things. Even with all the Magnolia finery, I only bought two things—and only by the extreme insistence of my family and the repeated chorus that it was my birthday. I did buy a dozen or so gifts, but for the purpose of this story, we are not counting those. (Wink wink!)

As she hovered and hollered and we repeated, I got a little sick to my stomach. I have known this single scripture longer than any other, but I realized at that moment, sitting in that chair, I had been selfishly disobedient to this command every day and every single way of my life.

It is not things I want. I want for peace and wisdom. I want to see a different image in the mirror and a different number on the scale. I want to know the future. I want the prize but not the process. I want heaven without dying and health without trying. I want it all.

These words and my list of wants ran through my mind like a freight train. I realized each syllable painted a picture of distrust and disgust, distrust of my Creator and disgust with myself. The conference was roughly eight hours. I easily spent the first four in complete turmoil. It was terrible.

The Holy Spirit corrects and convicts, and He was having a heyday with me. But He also teaches. He had not brought me all the way to Houston to slap my hand; He had brought me to mold my heart. He says, "Do not want," but read on. We shall not want because we do not have to.

The wants are born out of distrust. A sheep trusts the shepherd. The shepherd protects and provides. He sees ahead and watches behind. He keeps his sheep from their enemies, and he cares deeply about where they go.

The shepherd wants his sheep to know they are cared for and safe. He wants them to know that he understands what they need and that he will be there for them. He wants them to see they are all unique, and he foresees what that uniqueness will yield, where it will take them, and the dangers it implies.

Want is the double-edged sword of dissatisfaction and distrust. It thrusts us into self-strained motivation and the ever-emptying glass of performance. It forgets we are made to want Him and Him alone, and that is the want that satisfies. There is incredible freedom in knowing we do not have to want.

I embraced the freedom that day. The freedom of wanting Him above all else truly aligns every path, satisfies every need, and fulfills every hope. There were so many reasons God had me in that place. So many pieces of my heart found peace. And so many times I wondered if I didn't get this one right, Psalm 23, AKA Christianity 101. How many foundational truths was I missing?

Let's talk about some. Let's reacquaint ourselves with who we are in Christ, what that means, and where we are going. It is all there in scripture. It is all there like buried treasure viewed through clear water. We can see it, but we have to reach in and pick it up. We have to hold it and let the weight of it caress our hands and hearts. It is deposited for a return—gift for glory and love for more love.

It is strong enough, big enough, and wide enough to hold us and be the undergirding for the path we take. The foundation, scripture, and our faith in its truth is the first and perhaps the most important stop on our journey. He never disappoints, His truth never fails, and His friendship never forsakes. We must understand who we are and who we are in Christ.

In the back of this book, you will find prompts for each section. You might find it useful to conclude each of our six steps with the short exercises there. Know that I am praying for you as you journal and journey.

Our very first stop in our journey to fierce, foundation, rests in a tiny village called Whoville. What we think of God—or, more simply, who God is to us—as well as what God thinks of us are critically important. Who are we to God? It is an amazing study and truly one of the most humbling places we can live.

Here in Whoville, we will first think about who God is. I do not pretend to truly understand this, but please bear with me. You and I, like with our salvation, must work this out. The object of our affection, like the love of our life, must be known. We must spend time getting to know Him, developing a relationship with Him. It may sound strange. Welcome to my little corner of the world. I'm so glad you are here.

But as I write, I look at a beautiful chair at the end of my dining room table and pretend Christ is there. I want Him to be part of this. I want Him to be part of the process when I read the Bible. When I read passages of the Bible that I do not understand, I ask Him. He has an uncanny way of writing on hearts that I simply cannot explain or describe. I absolutely know with every part of my being He wants to be known.

How do you see God? For some of us, He is a kind and loving Father, and we attribute to Him some of the same qualities we love or loved about our fathers. Perhaps it is the love, the forgiveness, or the mercy and joy we find or found in our father's presence. For some, He is the father we never had or hoped we could have had.

Perhaps we see Him as Santa Claus, the object of our prayers resembling lists and petitions that sound very much like conditional demands. I love to pray; listening, however, is not my strong suit. To get to know Him, to really know Him, we have to silence ourselves. I don't know about you, but silence does not come easy. And listening? Well, let's just say I am learning.

If I had to write a class on God 101, Who God Is, I am confident I would look for the facts, the unfailing, guaranteed characteristics and promises of God. Perhaps you are venturing into scripture reading; possibly you have read scripture for years. Either way, grab a journal and a sharp pencil. I am very jazzed about sharp pencils when I write. Now start a list of the promises of God as you read them.

These promises reveal with the most amazing lens of clarity who God is. And, spoiler alert, estimates vary, but the promises are in the thousands, some say over seven thousand, you can take to the bank about our God!

So let's pretend you and I are going to meet for coffee every Saturday to find these promises. We will be reasonable, and our goal will be ten promises each week. We will make time for a muffin and plan for, let's say, one hour. We would meet for the next thirteen years. I personally would love this! Tea, coffee, muffins, or scones, you choose. Can you imagine how our image of God would mold and shift?

For practice, let's start in Psalm 27.

> The LORD is my light and my salvation—whom shall I fear? The LORD is the stronghold of my life—of whom shall I be afraid? When the wicked advance against me to devour me, it is my enemies and my foes who will stumble and fall. Though an army besiege me, my heart will not fear; though war break out against me, even then I will be confident. One thing I ask from the LORD, this only do I seek: that I may dwell in the house of the LORD all the days of my life, to gaze on the beauty of the LORD and to seek him in his temple. For in the day of trouble he will keep me safe in his dwelling; he will hide me in the shelter of his sacred tent and set me high upon a rock. Then my head will be exalted above the enemies who surround me; at his sacred tent I will sacrifice with shouts of joy; I will sing and make music to the LORD. Hear my voice when I call, LORD; be merciful to me and answer me. My heart says of you, "Seek his face!" Your face, LORD, I will seek. Do not hide your face from me, do not turn your servant away in anger; you have been my helper. Do not reject me or forsake me, God my Savior. Though my father and mother forsake me, the LORD will receive me. Teach me your way, LORD; lead me in a straight path because of my oppressors. Do not turn me over to the desire of

my foes, for false witnesses rise up against me, spouting malicious accusations. I remain confident of this: I will see the goodness of the LORD in the land of the living. Wait for the LORD; be strong and take heart and wait for the LORD.

This happens to be where my Bible in a year took me this morning, which by the way has been a huge help marrying Old and New Testaments, psalms, and proverbs. Our Psalm 27 list, with our notebook and sharpened or mechanical pencil, if you are fancy, would look something like this:

God is:

1. My light
2. My salvation
3. My reason to not fear
4. My fortress
5. My protector from danger
6. My defender
7. My army
8. My host in heaven
9. My concealer
10. My positioner, "hiding me in his sanctuary where I will be out of reach of my enemies"

Get the picture? He has so very much for us to discover. You see, as He paints this picture and creates the masterpiece that is you, me, and everyone, He wants us to be looking back at Him, trusting the strokes, color, temperature, and, more than anything, the process of it all. If He is all Psalm 27 says He is and so much more; He can, should, and is able to be our foundation.

Now then, let's not stamp our passport and leave Whoville too quickly. Who are we to Him? We will stand before Him, represent ourselves to Him, and answer for what we did, yes, but to get to the what, we have to understand the who.

Who are we to God? I wonder what comes to your mind: child, son, or daughter. How do we reconcile a holy, supernatural being adopting us into His family, care, and grace? We, dear reader, are allowed to sit at His table.

It all started so perfect, literally. Genesis 1:26 gives us His directive, "Let us, (the three in one) make human beings in OUR image, making them to reflect our nature."

Think of the power of this. The three—Father, Son, and Holy Spirit— mutually think, create, and design a being (you and me) that would reflect the nature, essence, perfection, and wonder of God. Can you imagine the discussion? Arms to hug and hold, legs to walk and run, and a system that consumes and cleanses. There would be a brain to understand the nature of it all and the nature about them and the heart. The heart, a machine that pumps, functions, and feeds. A soul that carries His breath.

Zipping back to Genesis 1:26, let's notice these two words, *reflect* and *nature*. Reflect does not mean resemble. We are physical bodies on this earth, not yet spiritual beings like Him. We derive intelligence from Him, not of course at His level, but some piece of the mind of Christ. We are creative people able to solve problems and make things that do wonderful acts. We can find solutions to problems and write poetry and prose. And most wonderful of all, we have His breath in our lungs. Our souls are the very extension of His eternity.

His nature, love, compassion, mercy, and grace are all somehow imparted to us in different measures for different purposes and with a kaleidoscope of passions that drive us to be the individual soldiers in God's army. Therefore our lives, work, manner, breath, beings, and purpose are all created and crafted by a holy God to reflect Him.

Extraordinary! Just think: every DNA, fingerprint, eye color, stature, and footprint are all different. They are diverse, and divinely designed for individual destinies.

Every one of us is a masterpiece in His eyes, and every masterpiece is put on this earth to point others to Him. As His, our secular work becomes holy work. Our chores become worship. Our relationships become reverent as we discover Him in the very fabric of who we are and all we do.

Who we are and who we are to Him is a piece of critical understanding to have this foundation of faith, to know His Word is true, and to understand the kinship He has created that goes so far beyond student and teacher and pastor and parishioner. "See what great love the Father has lavished on us, that we should be called children of God! And that is what we are! The reason the world does not know us is that it did not know him" (1 John 3:3).

Children of God

Children begin as babies. They are forged into being with complete and total dependence on their parent or caregiver for every facet of their lives outside of breath. They must be fed and clothed, and they must be protected.

This dependence is a model for our relationship with God. We are to depend on Him and so much more. He wants us to depend on Him. He never grows weary of our questions. His infinite patience and extraordinary love are the gifts of our supernatural parent.

In Romans 11, Paul uses the term *grafted* six times. He knew his audience. He knew they knew the olive tree trade. He knew they knew that a wild olive is grafted with a cultivated olive in order to become a better olive.

We, the wild ones, are grafted with God. Impossible! How does God come up with this? How is it that we breathe the breath of a holy, living, perfect God of the universe other than Him placing something beautiful into our ugly, wild, and rogue self? I don't get it. I will never get this kind of mercy, grace, and compassion, but the day I saw it, felt it, and truly believed it was the day I met my daughter.

I can't tell you when I knew we would adopt. It was a series of puzzle pieces that I could not see. As a child, I had these wonderful Asian dolls passed down to me through uncles that had served in World War II. I thought they were the most beautiful things in the world. When my aunt brought home her daughter from Korea, I was four years old. Daddy picked up this new family from the airport, and they came to live with us for a few weeks. I looked at that little girl as if she were the most beautiful, porcelain beauty I had ever seen. There was some magic in this instant family. She joined her brothers as if she had always been there.

We had the most extraordinary gift of two boys. I can remember coming home to our little house with our second son, Beau, and I recalled the prayers I had whispered, knowing if Beau were a boy, God was confirming our call. It was crazy when I think of it now. I gave God a condition, yet divine calls are rarely if ever conditional. They are inescapable pieces of who we are that must be held and followed to be known. We are never truly ourselves if we do not follow them. And we can never fully know the character of God if we do not stretch and strain to reach them.

I see this now. Well situated in my rearview mirror, but then and to be honest still, when I hear a call from God, the Sarai in me attempts to leave Him a voice mail. I explain how the whole thing will work or perhaps what would be the easiest path to get there. I ponder what I think I can and cannot do as well as the economic feasibility of each and every vestige of the plan. I am not sure why I do this. I am not sure why God hasn't completely thrown up His hands and moved on from my malarkey, but I know in my heart He is infinitely patient, and I am so grateful because He has had to be just that with me.

During my second pregnancy, I reasoned with God that having a biological girl would be nice too. Perhaps He meant that when he promised me a daughter. Maybe I misheard and possibly by some crazy accident of DNA she would have Asian eyes, as I had seen and dreamt about.

My labor with Beau was a full twenty minutes of the most excruciating pain I had ever felt. I remember politely screaming that I really wanted an epidural and the nurse shaking her head emphatically with the words, "You have missed your window." I believe my response was, "Open that window or kill me now."

Beau just turned seventeen years old. He entered this world like a rocket ship and still lives life that way. I took one look at his big blue eyes and his face that looked exactly like his Daddy's and knew when God says something, He means it. He proves it again and again, even for the most stubborn. I was not going to miss this window. I was not going to say two children were enough even with owning a business and working in ministry. It would have been so very easy to say that.

To miss the window? My goodness, we would have missed so much. We would have missed these two melodic joys we call our daughters, and I would have missed two journeys of faith that have meant everything to me.

I knew a place where some little fierce embers were burning. I didn't want to miss it. Bailey was six years old, and Beau not yet one when we started our path toward adoption. Brian was not on the same page. Word to the wise, adoption takes 200 percent commitment from both parties from start to finish. You have to start together. So when one is not quite on the same page or in the same place, you pray hard, really hard.

There was something so beautiful about the call. As much as I knew it was ours, I also knew it was not mine to convince Brian. There are jobs tailor-made for us and ones made for the Holy Spirit. This was definitely the latter.

I cannot tell you when, but there was a moment in those months as Brian was driving somewhere that the sun hit his windshield. The Lord spoke, "Your daughter is on the other side of the world." He called me. God had birthed our daughter in his heart, and we were suddenly both in. There was absolutely no going back. How do you love someone you have never met? You begin to dream, wonder, and pray for a child in God's care. You realize the child is in His garden, His olive grove, waiting to be grafted in.

That was step one. Steps two through twelve were finding the country, agency, and social worker and completing the reams of paperwork. Brian does not like paperwork. It is not his lane. It was true then and today. But he completed all of it, filed, refiled, sealed, and apostilled 100 percent of the paperwork. When people say adoptions are miraculous, this was truly one of our miracles. He astounded and amazed me.

Every day, with the internet still being new, he would sit on phone calls, make appointments, and draft and redraft. He was Superman in this process. I never doubted for one minute he would complete it. Holy missions have miracles woven in, and this was one of them.

The path to her home country, Kazakhstan, was hard. There were the mounds of paperwork and friends who didn't think we had the brightest of ideas. There was our family concerned about our safety and our little sons traveling so very far. There were the warnings that our boys would not be able to come into the orphanage, thus requiring another traveler to care for them while we visited. And there was the backbreaking, soul-searching cost. I am praying right now as your journey crosses those adopting, thinking of adopting, and praying about adopting. Love them well. It is gut-wrenching hard.

There was the blind referral and warning that this little face with whom I had fallen passionately in love with would not actually be in the orphanage. There was the flight from the capital to northeast Kazakhstan in a fifty-year-old, thirty-seat plane that dripped with the rain falling outside in the cabin.

There was the ride to the apartment where we were warned to not speak of our daughter to the director and to hide the photo hanging around my neck. There was the apartment with some eight locks on the door. There was the warning to never open the door unless the translator was knocking. We installed ourselves in the apartment, unpacked, and learned the schedule. At 9:45 the next morning and for seventeen mornings thereafter, we were to come outside, but only when we saw our driver and car to go to Lily's orphanage.

But then there was that moment. It was already late in the afternoon. As I folded clothes, I mentally picked out what I would wear to meet her the next day. I had packed what had amounted to camping supplies, which would be our dinner. The boys found their beds, and I was so ready to rest my jet-lagged heart. We had been told our first meeting would be the next day. Our coordinator and translator rushed into the kitchen. It was more James Bond than I cared for, with fur hats, fast Russian, and intrigue as they said in broken English, "We can go now."

Now? I had not changed. Two years and suddenly I had two minutes.

There were no questions, primping, or preparing; it was just a dash down the stairs into a van and more warnings. "Do not speak unless spoken to; do not act like you have seen her picture." Tears burned my eyes. The moment we had waited for and the little girl I had dreamed of were seconds away.

We raced upstairs to a small office. A Eurasian man walked in. He was both director and doctor. After small talk, the door opened. I saw my beloved girl in a plaid dress and crew cut with the shiniest eyes I had ever seen. The nurse, looking like something out of a commercial from the fifties with her white uniform, handed her to me.

Lily leaned back as if my body were the comfy chair she had been looking for, and her spiky crew-cut hair brushed under my neck. Her head filled the small of my neck absolutely perfectly. Her warmth covered me. She felt every inch a part of me. The doctor and nurse were obviously monitoring us, and both seemed surprised. Quickly it was translated that Lily was a very shy, introverted baby, one that did not go to strangers ever. "This was different," they said.

We felt a part of each other, the same way Bailey had filled my heart laying in his isolette minutes after his birth and Beau had filled my ears with the sweetest songs I had ever heard. Five years later it would all happen again as Ava Joy was handed to me in a Civil Affairs office. This child filled every pore of my being like marmalade filling crevices in bread. Two little adopted girls growing and completing my heart like our boys had done.

Yet there was a difference. There were not the nine months of physical growth where heartbeats and inches are measured. There was the journey of waiting, wondering, hoping, and quite literally a thousand prayers all in this moment. There was one soul joined with another, not through physical DNA but ethereal intertwining.

At that moment, I saw God in a different light. We are not born physically of the Father. We are born of His hand, heart, and mind and out of His love. I have two adopted girls, one from Kazakhstan and the other from China. They are blended and grafted in our family to make us stronger, to understand something of their culture, birthplace, and homeland.

We are grafted into God's family and called His children to strengthen us through His very Spirit, to better understand Him and His character, and to embrace the fact that this is not our home. Our adoptive Father places us in an earthly family to learn love and forgiveness, blessing and suffering, and beauty and grace until He takes us from this earthly home and welcomes us to His. He is Creator, Father, Protector, and Lover of our souls. His design, your DNA, your family, your gender, your country of origin, your passions, and your peculiarities are all fostered and formed by the hand of God.

Whether you feel grafted to your birth or adoptive family, you can know without a shadow of a doubt by confessing your sins to the Holy Savior that you are part of His family. Your love is a reflection of Him. Your talents are a masterpiece of the Master Designer (Ephesians 2:10). Your passions are a part of the plan of salvation for someone in your circle of influence.

Your faults, gaps, or mistakes is the place the Holy Spirit can fill. When He says we can do all things (Philippians 4:13), it is only to remind us that we need Him to do everything.

So we stand, you and I, dear one, on a foundation, our first step to *fierce.*

4

Inviting Him In

We went to the flea market this weekend. My sweet, little nine-year-old decided to wear flip-flops. It's August, and of course I didn't see this little fashion choice until we were well on our way to the first barn. We were at the fairgrounds, full of enough gravel to support a small city. Every few yards we would hear Ava Joy yell, "Hold on!" while she shook out her flippers.

Gravel is sturdy; gravel holds us up. The foundation of that flea market was absolutely secure, but those tiny pieces dancing in the souls of Ava's shoes distracted her from the fun of the day, the toys on every table, and the wonder of a million things she could not see because the gravel spoke louder.

I get it. I have had the privilege to teach women in and outside my church for a dozen or so years. In that time, I have heard literally hundreds of times, "When?"

- When I lose weight …
- When I retire …
- When my child …
- When my husband …
- When I can afford …

There are practical sides to every single one of those. I think I personally have said them all. Yet think of the garden. Jesus appointed his disciples to pray. He was about to face the single-most agonizing moments of His life. The disciples said, "After we nap …"

The time was and is now. You and I are navigating together. Our goal is fierce. The time is now. We have determined in our hearts where we are going and decided in our minds the destination. This is a holy journey, and as such, it will be fraught with obstacles. We have already discussed the obstacle of fear, but there are more.

You see, this is not our journey alone. We have not booked passage for you and me alone, but with the Holy Spirit as our guide. We must remember to invite Him. We must remember that He is with us and never leaves us. Above all else, we must invite Him into the path of the journey and the parts of our minds that resist our abilities to become fierce. The when most certainly is now, but how.

The devil is the derailer, distracter, and devourer of our dreams, courage, and destination. He will knock us off our paths with a whisper of doubt. He will convince us we lack confidence, skill, and wisdom. God, however, is the gap filler. I will not tell you this journey is easy. I will tell you with Jesus we can and will arrive at fierce.

We need Him. We need to invite Him in. Our Shepherd guides. We want Him along the road of our passions and purpose, but what about the dark places of doubt and ugly emotions? This is the gravel, the small places in our hearts that are hard and irritating but seem either unworthy of His attention or too unbecoming for His glance.

This idea of invitation is not a new one. He tells us in Psalm 23:2b–5a that we are invited.

> He leads me beside quiet waters, he refreshes my soul. He guides me along the right paths for his name's sake. Even though I walk through the darkest valley, I will fear no evil, for you are with me; your rod and your staff, they comfort me. You prepare a table before me in the presence of my enemies.

An invitation to His table of enemies, I have them. I am confident you do as well. The dark and the doubt, how do we invite Him there? What are your negative emotions?

Have you assumed, like me, that they are part of you? This is the natural reaction to life, disappointment, and failure. Are the "whens" hiding the why? "When I lose weight" is an easier statement than "I am afraid." "When my husband does this or that" might be covering the anger or sadness I experience every day. Anger, fear, guilt, and sadness are emotions and dark spaces we count as part of us. How we are wired. Our reasonable reaction to the revelry around us reveals the enemies within us. What if for a moment we travel to these places?

Dr. Allison Cook and Kimberly Miller give us this guidance,

> Having the Holy Spirit within doesn't automatically bring perfect peace and joy, however, because some parts of your soul can be stubborn and resist God's will. In any moment, you can choose whether to walk with the Spirit or to go your own way. Thankfully, you can play an active role in connecting the troubled parts of yourself to the Holy Spirit who dwells inside of you. You can invite him to be with them, and you can witness His power at work-in partnership with God. You can befriend and lead the unruly parts of your soul into an abundant life. (23)

If you have a negative emotion, a dark space you have long locked away, invite Him in. If you feel your time has passed, your failures too great, your sins too gross, your life too short, or your bank account too small, invite Him in. There is holy waiting, and there is earthly stalling. Discern the season you are in. God does not need us, but He amazingly, desperately, and extraordinarily wants us. Want Him back.

Sit at the table with your enemies. Let Him anoint your head with oil—this crazy oil. Did you know that sheep needed oil? Oil allowed their heads to graze off another sheep who decided to get in their space. Oil mended their wounds. Oil, by its very scent, kept the poisonous adders from biting them.

We too are covered with His protection and balm. We don't sit at the table unprotected. We sit at the table to be healed and unburdened and to take the hurting parts and move then to the healing posture God has. Your suffering is often where He nestles His ministry.

What distracts us from our foundation? The list is endless. The gravel in our lives is many and varied. The most avid Bible reader, the highest trained athlete, and the most gifted scholar become distracted from the work, the call, and the foundation.

For me, the distraction, the loss of focus, has not been as much without but within. It is not the events, big or scary or safe and sound, but my reaction to them is the emotional reaction, the self-narration, and the personal judgment that is far from the view I know that God holds of you and me.

> Praise be to the God and Father of our Lord Jesus Christ, who has blessed us in the heavenly realms with every spiritual blessing in Christ. For He chose us in him before the creation of the world to be holy and blameless in his sight. In love He predestined us for adoption to sonship through Jesus Christ, in accordance with his pleasure and will—to the praise of his glorious grace, which He has freely given us in the One he loves. In him we have redemption through his blood, the forgiveness of sins, in accordance with the riches of God's grace that he lavished on us. (Ephesians 1:3–8a)

Emotions created by God to show us His feelings for us are the same things that can seem like the gravel in our flip-flops waging war against the peace that He gives.

We cope, right? We feel and move on as if the bags of our feelings are the necessary evil to carry as we lead a life for Christ. They are numerous and nasty—anger or envy or failure or fear. Your poison is not your choice; it is picked for you.

Until very recently, I thought emotions—good, bad, and otherwise— were part of the package of life, in and out of control. We love to love, and the Bible tells us not to hate. We are caught in the dilemma of wanting to grow some emotions and controlling some others. And we often do not understand why some emotions seem to skip over us and others seem to want to sink us. These emotions are the ammunition of the heart and the battlefield of the mind.

I read a blog by Dr. Alison Cook when my heart was hurting. It wasn't grief or aching melancholy; it was a gnawing gravel-in-the-shoe type of emotion. I could shake it off 90 percent of the time, but I was weary of it. I was absolutely aware it was distracting me from more meaningful thoughts. It was the thief of my peace, and I was sick and tired of it. In *Boundaries for the Soul*, Cook and Miller take us through a step-by-step process of navigating emotions to a state of acceptance, learning their source and even befriending them.

These enemies, our negative emotions, are invited to the table. Us, the Holy Spirit, and the emotions that trouble us. The invitation requires something of us. It requires the Holy Spirit to point us to the source of the emotion. His presence is a revealer and redeemer.

My invitation was into a space of envy. I am not proud of that, but in the spirit of transparency and truth, this is where I began. Naming the emotion was easy; discerning its source felt impossible. It literally had always been part of me, like hazel eyes and wavy hair, but the thought of unseating it was too appealing to not send an invitation.

What is yours? The emotion or emotions that continue to stifle, frighten, or discourage you? Write it down in the corner of this page or portion of your heart. This was my experience. I pray it leads you to yours.

Psalm 23:5 talks of a "table prepared with our enemies." My gravel, my negative emotion, was envy. I wanted a life different from my own. I wanted to be an easy-breezy person who didn't take things to heart, didn't feel she had to prepare five years for a five-minute meeting, or had to strive, strive, strive to be smarter, thinner, wiser, and stronger. If one of your negative emotions is envy, welcome to my world. If not, still read on. The process and the pain are the same. We are together. Let's forge on.

I focused on the envy, trying to figure out if there was a starting point. For the first time, I asked Jesus into this space, and I asked Him to help me learn if there had been a beginning point. James 4:8 promises, "Draw near to God and He will draw near to us." We open up the house of our heart without shutting the closet, bedroom, or basement doors. We let Him look, dwell, and then live, see, and know. He already does, but we acknowledge Him and give Him permission to look in the cupboards.

Jesus invited people. We need to reciprocate and invite Him back. I asked Jesus most sincerely to show me where this envy had come from, earnestly hoping if I could find the source, I could somehow navigate its seeming hold on me. I wanted to live outside of the boundaries of its walls. I was absolutely convinced that if I could stop striving for even just a few moments, I might live in the peace of all God was doing and had done. Exhale envy; breathe in grace. What do you need to exhale? I am praying for you now.

"Curiosity and compassion" (*Boundaries for the Soul*, 26) are the guideposts we use. Condemnation seemed to be my go-to, so I was willing to trade those as I asked Jesus to take me on this journey.

As I prayed, the Lord led me to my three-year-old self, three-year-old Cathy. I had pigtails and navy-blue Keds with white laces. I was outside virtually every day. Memories of the backyard were as real as if I were standing there now—the birdbath, the gigantic lilac bush, Mama's clothesline, and my best friend, Dot, and I picking a thousand bouquets of weeds.

Next door lived Dot. Dot was older, thinner, smarter, and three years my senior. She was exactly twice my age and therefore twice as good. In my eyes she was brilliant. She came up with the best ideas. She in her sweet friendship became a role model for me. By the time I was four, Dot had become my idol.

She seemed to roll out of bed and into the backyard. Her hair seemed to just fall into place. Her mom was not a stickler for pigtails like mine. My hair to this day has never decided if it is straight or curly. It has an odd, unruly wave. Most mornings it lands in one big barrette. I will go to glory trying to train my hair.

Dot, on the other hand, had straight, calm, happy hair. She also, or at least in my four-year-old opinion, pulled on clothes that looked trendy in the elementary school style that I could only wish for. Dot was thin; I was round. Dot seemed to have no agenda but always had a plan. Dot was both creative and carefree. Dot was who I wanted to be. I didn't exactly know that then, but I know the day it occurred. Jesus brought me that. He brought me back.

Due to my four-year-old idolatry, I would wait to see Dot outside. I would look at how her hair was styled and admire it. I would pay attention to what she was wearing and look to model her. On one particular summer day, Dot came out in shorts and a white button-down blouse. I did not own a white button-down blouse. Funny, I can show you at least three in my closet today, although until this reflection, I had no idea where this reverence came from.

I marched into the kitchen and told my mother exactly what I was looking for. Mother, forever practical, reminded me I did not own a blouse matching that description; nor would "we go out to play in white." Then her directive came, "Go out and play, like Dot."

And there it was. I wanted to be just like her. I wanted to be her. Somewhere in the quirkiness of a four-year-old brain, this envy had started, and when my precious mother chided me to "be like her," my fate was sealed.

Let's be real here. Moms do this. I do this. I see a great character trait in another child or mom, for that matter, and I tell people, including the persons in my house who are my own children, whom I admire and why. And perhaps, just perhaps, I have said out loud, "I wish you would be like …" Mothering is a work in progress. I am not sure, but I think we finish in heaven.

Envy, like so many other negative emotions, can be the stepping-stone to great healing and amazing self-awareness, and it can become building blocks to creating allies out of enemies. We must, however, never ever underestimate the role of the devil. We give him footholds, and believe me, he has big feet that want to stamp us out. He is not the irritating third-grader that pulls our braids. He is in it to win and to kill. "The thief comes ONLY to steal and kill and destroy; I have come that they may have life, and life to the FULL" (John 10:10, emphasis added).

The devil will derail, but let us remember the derailment of our journey, the when-I, the what-if, and the if-only is a place we must stop. We must stop and invite God in to reveal the true reason for the objection. We stop and invite Him. Is God showing me something He wants me to learn? Or am I following the path of idolatry, paved so many years ago that being me meant being more like someone else?

When I invited Jesus into this space, so many things happened. Parts of my heart, quiet, unopened parts, were available to learn from. They were not all pretty or fun places to visit. They were spaces I needed to see, hear, and feel again. They were places I thought I would never know again, and yet they were as familiar as my name. I realized God was crazy about little

Cathy. I realized He never intended me to understand this sweet friendship or the words of my mom in a way that would hurt, harm, or harass me for so many years.

I asked Him two things: to unburden the sense that I was less but also to release me from the striving to be more. By asking Him in, He delicately showed me where my focus had shifted off the miracle, the Ephesians 2:10 masterpiece, into mundane mimicry.

Perhaps your pain, your emotion, does not rest in envy. Maybe it is sadness, fear, or anger. Possibly you know exactly when it started, the moment or day, of the death, loss, or abuse.

Beloved, invite Jesus into the space that feels less than holy and allow Him to make it so. When the sinner confesses, he becomes righteous. When the hurt walks into this space, the healing begins. Your ability to respond with something beautiful lies in the bearing of your soul to the Creator of your soul. He already knows, but He desperately wants to stand with you in it and through it and, if not to make sense out of it, to bring some healing and wholeness to it.

And perhaps, just perhaps, we need some professional help. This does not eliminate God. It allows Him to express Himself through the words of a counselor or therapist. I have been amazed at what these professionals can do.

We are a triad of mind, body, and spirit. We cannot have one without the other; we cannot have an action without a reaction. Our minds must react in symphony with our spirit. Our bodies crave the discipline of the other two.

My back doctor told me earlier this year I should consider not eating gluten, sugar, or excessive sodium. I was not a good candidate for surgery, and fortunately for him, he caught me on a good bad day. A bad day is a day my back is debilitatingly bending me over; a good bad day is one I can actually decide to do something about it without dozens of self-pitying thoughts, perhaps a few but not a dozen.

I saw this doctor by accident. We had tried all the shots, and through the hard work of my loving husband, we had collectively decided on stem cell therapy. We arrived ready to talk cells. Only this doctor said quite sheepishly that he puts stem cells "everywhere but not the spine." The appointment had quite frankly been made in error. Obviously he admitted the nurses at the desk had misheard my request, but out of my desperation and his apologies, he listened to Brian and me for a long time. He said, "If you were my wife, this is what I would do."

They were hard words, as I am not in love with much that is not quick and guaranteed, but there was a divine sense that nothing really occurs by accident. The path has been a hard one but one to wholeness. It has required retraining.

Today, I don't go near the soda fountain at 7-Eleven. I cannot bring even the healthiest treats from Trader Joe's into my home if they have a lot of sodium. And sugar and I, well, we still celebrate birthdays and Grandma Candy's cherry pie, as I don't think God or I could have it any other way.

But this retraining is Holy Spirit work. The mental retraining and rethinking of ways we have reacted for days or years is work into which we must invite God. And guess what? He shows up. And to no one's surprise, except perhaps my own, He shows up abundantly.

He shows up in the space where the negative emotion lives. He is not surprised. He sits and observes, and He reconciles what feels ugly to the beauty only He can create. What felt shameful, hidden, or dark is brought into the light of Him. He does not disparage it or cause it to disappear. He defines where it came from. He explains its meaning, and He allows us the friendship of our former enemy.

Like so much of what only He can do, it defies understanding, and yet we know the peace that follows the learning that inevitably comes is a gift.

It is the acknowledgement of the emotion, the acquaintance with its Creator, the acquiescence to its source and purpose, and the embrace of something more beautiful.

Be ready, beloved. This invitation and this work are wonderful.

5

Hospitality

Hospitality is mentioned over a dozen times in the Bible. Hospitality is the receiving of those whether we know them or not in a friendly or generous way. It is what Jesus did. It is a key to sharing life and the gospel and to learning.

What does holiday mean to you? What does hospitality mean? For years—and I mean well over half my life—I have associated hospitality with work, that is, the building up to entertain, the house, the meal, and the wardrobe. This started early.

As children, our Christmas began roughly one week before the actual day. We were released from school, and it was as if a magical clock chimed for the holidays to begin. As little children, Mother would take us to pick out a tree until the day Daddy discovered what he called "the Barney Fife" tree stand. Right next to a sheriff's office, we would go out early in the evening and find our treasure. Next would come ornaments, candlesticks, garland, and then the nativity. I can still see every inch of it.

Christmas Eve, Daddy would go to the store for all sorts of foods we didn't typically eat, lunch meats that were typically too expensive to buy and chips and dip that were typically too fattening to eat. Herring? The jury is still out on why he bought that, but Mama seemed to love it.

He would set up a little buffet, and our dearest friends and closest neighbors would come and go all evening. Daddy would tend a fire in the fireplace, and Mother would be refilling the platters of delights and baskets of chips. Sometime late in the evening, we would take a drive. Our entire neighborhood would light the streets with luminaries. It was extraordinary.

Daddy would drive every street looking for any lane that had a curved path so we could witness the splendor of the lights winding up the road. We would give each street a score, and if one house had not participated, we would title the owner discourteously as "Scrooge."

Returning home, we would have just missed Santa Claus by the most unfortunate timing. One year in particular, a piece of red fur had been left in the closed door as if his escape were so delightfully quick that he had shut the door on his coat. This has remained in Boswell folklore for my entire life.

Mom and Daddy's closest friends would sit and watch us open our gifts. There was riotous laughter, hugs, and the deepest joy I knew as a child. My mom was a thoughtful and wonderful shopper. She had a beautiful sense of taste for our particular loves and interests. We would go to bed well past midnight holding something incredibly dear to our hearts.

The next day, Christmas Day, had a decidedly different tone. After Mama passed on to heaven, we became the hosts of Christmas dinner. The mornings would start early. To this day, I wonder how my Mama did it. She had to be exhausted. We knew we were. Grace and Cold Duck. Daddy would have a few bottles of the latter chilling in the fridge.

Mom instilled in us a great love for family. Her brother and sisters would arrive. Mother made sure there was plenty of delicious German food and quite literally something on the table everyone loved. If we were seating for seventeen, we could easily have seventeen different dishes on the table, a delicious and personalized favorite for everyone at the table. I don't ever remember my mom sitting down for that meal. She, with her holiday apron, would be running, popping up and down, filling and refilling, and heating and reheating. She rarely complained, but she looked so very tired. I am sure I was little to no help. I would rush my presents upstairs and steal away to play. I defined my agenda by the holiday, certainly not the hospitality. I framed hospitality with obligation. I looked at the work and weary of it all and forged a negative perspective that followed me for years.

Don't get me wrong. I absolutely loved the finished project: a clean house, a lovely meal, lit candles, and shining china. All these things speak to me. They are very much a love language, but the time before? I believe it would be called hostility, not hospitality. I found the work hard and questioned my motives. Did the house have to look a certain way or the food be a certain class above our family norm?

I so want to be the easy-breezy hostess, the one on Instagram that can whip up food for twenty. She has the right stuff in her pantry, fashionable clothes in her closet, and salon-ready hair. And she serves with no grease on her shirt and no pans in her sink. I am not her. I plan and make lists, and I have often forgotten to enjoy the moment, waiting to hear the recap on the meal.

Some things—well, everything—changes when we pray. These things change because the Holy Spirit is so gracious and relentlessly pursues the ways He can show off His grace, the ways that will specifically speak to us.

In the very same week, some twenty or so years ago, it was around the holidays. We were invited by two different dear friends for two different dinners. The first, a lifelong friend, had a fabulous table and food. There was china, napkin rings, coffee in formal decanters, and homemade everything. It was absolute perfection. I will admit a wee bit of the evening I spent wondering if I could pull this off. Remember I navigate toward envy?

A few nights later, it was other dear friends and another meal. They had a store-bought buffet, paper plates, plastic forks, and pops in the fridge. And guess what? It was perfection. It was everything my heart needed that night, just like the three nights before. It was lovely people making a lovely space. Period.

That is hospitality. I still love a straightened home, but I rarely dust. I like a nice meal, but Trader Joe's is my secret lover. I still love a great cup of coffee, but I have learned my husband makes a better pot of coffee than I ever could, and by the greatest of wonders, he loves helping me. It doesn't make me any less of a hostess, but I had to learn to ask and adjust to the fact that because Mama didn't do it, it did not make it wrong.

Hallelujah. Dear one, ask a friend. Find one or a dozen people who want to be present in your presence over coffee or iced tea or chips and salsa. It is a gift. Invitations lead to hospitality. Inviting Jesus leads to a shared space for you and Him. In that shared space, we can ask, receive, speak, and listen. We can shout and surrender, and He remains. We can depart from despair and welcome the holiness of a holiday with Him.

When I invited Jesus into my envy, He stayed. In the dark and into the light, He will remain. He needs to be part of this journey to fierce without reservation. No area of our hearts can be off limits, and our souls can be confident in the welcome of Him. Our relegation of Jesus to when we are ready, have prayed, or gone to church is the exact opposite of His life.

He came for the sick. That is us. He came for the lonely, us as well. He came for the sinner. Let's all raise our hands. He is not surprised by us or our stuff. Let's welcome Him in. Let's experience Him walking and talking through our lives. Let us not relegate Him to Sunday mornings or quiet times. Let us invite Him in knowing we don't have to primp or prepare, but just experience His presence.

6

Experiencing His Presence

I wonder where you have experienced Jesus. I wonder what you have seen, heard, or felt that you have said, "Only God."

My husband finds Him at the piano. My friend Jodi finds him while listening to worship music. My friend Patty finds Him when bringing macaroni and cheese to anyone she knows or loves. Jesus is in those noodles, and anyone in Batavia, Illinois, will give you an amen.

My friend Penny finds Him while loving her neighbors, investing in those God places next door and across the street. My friend Dawn finds Him in snapdragons and the Swiss Alps. My friend Denice finds Him in the sunsets over the ocean. My friend Candy brings Him to every conversation, guiding and loving through her words. My friend Holly finds Him on Parisian streets. My friend Heather finds Him in praying for others.

My friend MaryBeth finds Him in helping, creating, and giving. My friend Susan finds Him in sharing the gospel and studying with friends. My friend Evon finds Him in delivering bouquets to her silver-haired lovelies. My friend Mary Ann finds Him in writing checks for the destitute. How about you?

> It would seem that Our Lord finds our desires not too strong, but too weak. We are half-hearted creatures,

fooling about with drink and sex and ambition when
infinite joy is offered us, like an ignorant child who wants
to go on making mud pies in a slum because he cannot
imagine what is meant by the offer of a holiday at the sea.
We are far too easily pleased. (Lewis 26)

What is your holiday at sea? The birth of a child? The feeling of true
love? The Grand Canyon? The forgiveness of someone you have betrayed?
We sense something more than ourselves. Someone, Jesus, has joined
us on the journey. The beauty beyond our imagination, the joy bursting
our heart, or the redemption we didn't think possible is experiencing His
presence. Should we, as Lewis poses, content ourselves with mud pies when
we have at our heart's grasp a "holiday at sea"? What if the experience could
be daily, moment to moment? It is possible. It is resetting our minds to the
possibility of constant presence and continual companionship.

For Nicholas Herman, it was a barren tree, one he knew well. Sitting
in his yard in the cold of winter, this familiar tree greeted him from his
window. He looked at the tree without its leaves, yet knowing in the spring,
the tree would quite literally spring back to life. It would be radiant, green,
and blossoming. Somewhere around 1630, God used that tree to cause
Nicholas to understand for the first time that God is a God of abundant
grace, a God that takes what is seemingly dead and brings it to life.
Nicholas knew at that moment God had more for Him.

Born into a very poor family in Lorraine, France, Nicholas, without
professional prospects, joined the army. Regular meals and pay seemed the
logical next step in his late teens. But then an injury returned him home.
As he glanced at that tree, Nicholas experienced God for the first time. He
knew if God could create this kind of beauty in a dead-looking twig of a
tree, how much more beauty did He have for him?

Nicholas joined the Carmelite Monastery in Paris and became Brother
Lawrence. He endeavored for the rest of His life to find God in the most
mundane of tasks, to converse with God in the silence of his life, to know
God as his dearest friend, and to dedicate even the smallest of his thoughts
and tasks to the company of his Savior.

He wrote sixteen letters that would become the work, *Practicing the
Presence of God*. It seems mystical at first, but only if we forget to whom

Brother Lawrence prayed and to what he dedicated his life. He entertained angels as he scrubbed, cleaned, and cooked, causing his work to become worship. His superiors noticed the difference in him. The other monks recognized it as well. He did not just study and pray; he lived, ate, and worked with the constant companion of the Holy Spirit. It was noted of him that his soul had "come to its own place of rest" (*Christianity Today*, "Brother Lawrence").

Do we not crave the very same? We do not serve a hidden God. We serve a God that displays Himself if—and only if—we have eyes to see. Brother Lawrence developed that vision, and I am convinced we can too. It takes some trial and error and a dash of discipline, but this very simple practice takes prayer to presence, work to worship, and fear to fierce.

C. S. Lewis wrote, "The moment you wake up each morning … all your wishes and hopes for the day rush at you like wild animals. And the first job of each morning consists of shoving them all back; in listening to that other voice, taking that other point of view, letting that other, larger, stronger, quieter life come flowing in" (198).

Are you taming wild animals? Yep, me too. The animals are the thoughts that compete for space in our minds and move us so far from peace. That fear becomes our frame. These thoughts tell us it is not going to be okay, God has forgotten, and, the *pièce de résistance*, we are in charge and it is all up to us. It feels that way, doesn't it? Filling gaps and plugging holes? I don't have enough fingers, toes, or wisdom. Yet we know who does.

So did Frank Laubach. Frank Laubach lived in the twentieth century, spending much of his life serving as a missionary in the Philippines. When I think of Brother Lawrence, I can excuse my lack of zeal for seeking the presence of God since I don't live in a monastery. I don't know quiet. Much of my life is noisy. Yours too? But Laubach probably walked a harder, noisier life than you and I combined. He worked tirelessly promoting literacy, and additionally he dedicated his life to the souls of the Philippine people. His was not an easy life. I am guessing yours is not either.

I am guessing if you have picked up this book, you desire to be fierce in a life where fear, frustration, or lack of faith has tried to tear down the foundation you had when you were a child or first knew the Lord. The "I can do anything because He strengthens me" (Philippians 4:13) has become "I can do a few things well and really stink at most everything else."

Somewhere along the road, we took ownership. The innocence and dependence of childhood become the brazen independence of adolescence, which morphs into the required maturity of adulthood. Dependence on Jesus becomes a mélange diluted by education, ego, or cultural ethos. We are the multitaskers, the makers and shakers of our lives. And we lose the One who gave us this life, offering it as a gift, not a gavel.

We cannot experience the life-giving, soul-saving, righteous refreshment of the Holy Spirit one or two days a week while we attend church and expect to live the life God has called us to. Church is simply a filling station. Life empties; He fills.

Laubach came to the work of Brother Lawrence, knowing in the trials of serving he needed more. He needed God not only in church and his work, but moment by moment, day by day, in the center of the hardest task or greatest triumph. He needed to redecorate where God sat in the rooms of his heart.

By the time Laubach picked up the sixteen letters of Brother Lawrence, three hundred years had passed. The ideas were not new, yet like you and I, Pastor Laubach did not work in a monastery. He worked in a foreign land with a foreign language. I feel much the same. We all bear the passport of heaven. If we have accepted Jesus Christ as our Savior and confessed our sins, we become righteous. Righteous in His eyes and in our hearts, we become citizens of heaven.

To travel on the road to fierce, we build a foundation. We invite Him, and we must experience His presence. But how? Laubach took the experiences of Lawrence and gave us the practical approaches he used to bring God into his moments, his minutes.

I am not sure we can all do all of these, but perhaps one will whisper to your heart. The Holy Spirit has a heart language. He speaks and then repeats. He causes a scripture to jump from the page to our eyes. He prompts a friend to speak light where we only felt darkness. He causes beauty to be born where ugliness lived. When He moves in and our perspective shifts, there is no explanation other than Jesus. I am saying a prayer just now that one of these clues will be your way of discovering more of Jesus.

Think of something mundane you do. I am a mama of four. I could write a dissertation on the mundane things mamas do. Think of something you do almost every day. Your mundane may be driving the kids to school or filling the coffee pot with water. Mine may be folding the laundry or loading the dishwasher. Maybe it's your commute to work or walk to class.

Pick one of these things. Think of it as a daily time you will dedicate to the Holy Spirit and imagine God sitting or standing, folding, or riding with you. Think of this one single activity as your newfound time with Him. It is your gift to yourself.

Believe me here, you will come to crave it and treasure it. Discover Him in that place, let your mind question Him, and listen for His answer. Thank Him for the mundane, and I guarantee it will feel miraculous.

When do you read the Word? I am a morning person. I love the quiet of it. Those precious minutes and, on rare occasions, hours feel like something of a privilege, a hiatus from the schedule and seriousness of life. I sit at my dining room table. I inherited from my mother that the dining room and living room should be relatively orderly. Don't ask me about dust or dust bunnies. Let's just say we aim for order. Asking for a friend, is dusting really necessary? If your answer is yes, please do not let me know.

I turn a blind eye to dishes and email, and for some space of time, I sit and read. I ask Him to sit with me. He gets the head of the table. If I don't understand a verse or wonder why it is included, I ask. It seems odd, but it is His Word, and by asking His meaning or definition, a holy harmony takes shape. His Word is timeless, yet its meaning wanders down our specific path on a certain day, revealing its truth for our particular moment.

Where do you sit? Do you have a spot for reading and prayer? It is important and holy. It is your time with Him alone. We agree we can talk and travel with Him throughout the day, but this time dedicated to His Word is richer when it is not rushed. It is purposed when it is placed. It can be a table, bed, couch, or corner. I have an old suitcase I bought at a garage sale where I keep my notebooks and devotionals. It keeps order to the ebbs and flows of my reading materials. If you do not have your place, pray and find one. Then create a time and a routine with coffee or candles.

It sounds easy and lovely, and it is, but it is also something we must fight for. Absolutely everything in life, from babies to Zulily, will vie for your attention. The juice is squeezing the day for this first before everything clouds the mind or calendar.

Jesus pondered both the question and the answer. All the miracles, healings, and love poured out, and His people still did not see. He said in John 10:25–26, "The miracles I do in my Father's name speak for me, but you do not believe because you are not my sheep." He then in verse 27 describes the differentiator. "My sheep LISTEN to my voice; I know them, and they follow me" (emphasis added).

Notice that He does not say my sheep talk to me every day. My sheep get on their knees before bed. My sheep keep a prayer journal. Rather He says, "my sheep, my people, and my children; I know them because they listen." Don't we want that posture? The position of listening instead of listing? His presence affords us that grace.

A third suggestion is to whisper Jesus as we see people. This simple practice is the calling of His name in our heart as we see people, to invite Him into the space to open our eyes to them as His creation, to open our hearts to their situation or pain, and to open our ears to actually listen to their words. We whisper a prayer as we start a conversation. I am convinced this practice is an invitation to wisdom and patience. We live and breathe; we fight and fret in the natural. And yet every single moment of every single day, there is coexisting in the supernatural, unseen world. Glimpses of glory start with prayer.

He tells us He inhabits the praises of His people. Do you have a hymn, the one that marches scripture through melody? Sing it, hum it, and dance to it. It can be yours and His sacred anthem.

Finally let Him be your very last thought in the evening, and perhaps He will surprise you as the subject of your dreams. My dear friend Pennie taught me to go through the alphabet, thanking God for twenty-six different things with each letter. Gratitude is a transformative practice. It seeks to testify to His goodness and searches to find His grace. It is a light that squelches even the darkest of days. There is always something for which we can be grateful.

Twenty-six will become twenty dozen, and soon this time, the before bedtime will become time at the altar where we sacrifice a few moments of sleep for incredible peace. I have struggled to sleep for a hundred different reasons, but this simple practice has been my very aid to rest. I rarely get through the alphabet, and yet my dreams are sweeter and my rest richer.

Pastor Frank Laubach recognized the American church had started marking God on the calendar. Wednesday perhaps and Sunday mornings for sure, God could be checked off for the week. These times—these wonderful times of fellowship, stewardship, and discipleship—are life-giving for the believer and nonbeliever alike, but they are simply the filling up of the clay jar that is to be poured out every single day. Laubach desired more for himself and the church. He began to play what became known as the game of minutes, literally dedicating a moment of every hour to thoughts of God. Laubach reflects,

> The notion that religion is dull, stupid and sleepy is abhorrent to God, for He has created infinite variety and He loves to surprise us. If you are weary of some sleepy form of devotion, probably God is as weary of it as you are. Shake out of it, and approach Him in one of the countless fresh directions. When our minds lose the edge of their zest, let us shift to another form of fellowship as we turn the dial of the radio. Every tree, every cloud, every bird, every orchestra, every child, every city, every soap bubble is alive with God to those who know his language. (11)

On some days, he would use that minute to relieve someone's suffering or look at an image of Him. It is quite literally the surrendering of seconds for a new and profound, divine intimacy. It is not easy. The best rarely is. But it is incredibly life-changing and peace-giving. Give Him moments; He will fill hours. Give Him space; He will fill hearts. He is absolutely the most cherished friend. Susan Lenzkes said,

> Certain friends have a way of setting up residence in us. They march into some barren room of our heart and hang cheery curtains, scatter soft rug, dot the walls with framed prints of tender and whimsical moments then set about building a cozy fire beside two sink-back-and-stay-awhile chairs. We may not always know exactly when such friends moved in, but we are so very grateful they did. (*Women's Devotional Bible*, 249)

Rejoice

I am an NFL football fan. I have never learned to love college football, but if you give me a Sunday afternoon with my Chicago Bears, this girl is this side of heaven: happy.

I love the sport. I love the three hours of dedicating to something my daddy taught me to love. These days I text my oldest as we ride the wave of a great defense and a less than great offense. When our boys in blue are down, we look for a game-changer, a pick six, an old-style runback, or a crazy call by the refs.

This is joy. Okay, joy is way more than this, but I love a good football analogy. So what is the way more than this? I am so glad you asked. Joy is a noun defined as "a feeling of great happiness" (Merriam-Webster).

Joy is mentioned well over a hundred times in the Bible. The word *rejoice* is referenced over two hundred times. One could conclude because we have joy, we should rejoice. Rejoice is the literal action verb of joy. It is the showing or feeling of joy. "Let us fix our eyes on Jesus…, who for the joy set before Him endured the cross, scorning its shame, and sat down at the right hand of the throne of God" (Hebrews 12:2).

I love that word *fix*. Fix, focus, and pay attention. This joy, if we can fixate on that, is the end of the story, the redeeming nature of God, the love He pours out, and the mercy He refreshes every morning. We can do this. We can reach the finish line. We can do that hard thing staring us down at this very moment.

These hard things: the relationship that has gone wrong, that child who has your heart in pieces, the bank account that is more empty than full, or the sin that only you know about. He knows and sees, and He is still crazy in love with us. Our reaction, dear one, is only to rejoice.

Paul wrote it this way,

> Rejoice in the Lord always. I will say again. Rejoice! Let your gentleness be evident to all. The Lord is near. Do not be anxious about anything, but in everything, by prayer and petition, with thanksgiving, present your requests to God. And the peace of God, which transcends all understanding will guard your hearts and minds in Christ Jesus. (Philippians 4:4–7)

Don't we just want this? Don't we want the always, everyday, every-moment, every-situation joy? There is more here—more than wanting, the hope of joy, or even the promise of joy, which Paul clearly states is our commandment.

Joy is a game-changer. It is the NFL fan's guide to loving the Chicago Bears. The Bears don't win enough. The Bears have disappointed me more Sundays than I can share. But there's the joy of watching them and hollering with my sons and husband. Having a halftime of chips and hummus is joy. It is the experience of the game.

We, you and I, experience a life shared. We know through faith our ultimate destination. Past the destination of fierce is our home in heaven. We choose then how we will walk, the reaction we will have, the feeling we will give others, and the space we will share. Do we rejoice in this space?

I believe 100 percent of the Bible. I believe it is the infallible word of the Lord; the living, breathing spoken words of God; and the essential peace to the Christian life. The Bible says in the last days, "love of most will grow cold" (Matthew 24:12b).

Like me, I am sure you see frosted hearts all around you—hearts that have not met Jesus, hearts that used to know Him, hearts that have built a wall of hostility toward Him and to those who bear His name. And some preach the Word, yet it is a different word than I read. What we read as black and white now seems blurred to grey. It is a prophetic change in this time and in our world. It is one that should not surprise but grieve us. We must hold fast, not only to truth but to joy, as we find more arguing than agreement, more hate than love, and more confusion than compassion.

All who disagree or agree or believe or not, we all resemble each other in virtually every way. We eat together; we work together. We go to ball games and vintage markets. We raise our kids and fight the fight, but only the battles look different depending on the playbook. I am convinced that joy is the game-changer.

I met a woman some years ago who talked about interruptions. She talked about how when she missed a plane, she knew Jesus had something better. She talked about when God had not allowed a dream, He was writing something more divine. She was the very definition of joy. I am convinced our testimonies are not just what we say, how we live, or even how we act, but more so, our testimonies are how we react.

I am not at my loveliest when things don't go my way. I get angry when life seems unfair and I see the good guys losing. I have never welcomed suffering, and I am confident I never will. Yet scripture commands our reaction in joy.

Let's define joy beyond Webster for just a moment. Jon Piper provides the most eloquent and complete definition of joy I have ever read. He describes joy in *Desiring God* as four distinct yet divinely tied elements, "Joy is a feeling, in the soul, produced by the Holy Spirit which exists in the world and in the Word."

In four unique and simple phrases, Piper gives us the four foundations of joy. It is clearly an emotion, but more than happiness, it exists in the soul. It is not created or crafted by us, but rather the Holy Spirit draws us a map to it through His Word and in the world.

I was just in the Carolinas. When you order tea there, you get some of the sweetest, best tea in the world. I know me some tea. I can brew you some Earl Grey that you will long remember, but without asking in the Carolinas, my big iced glass was filled with sweet tea. You know they are using the same tea bags and boiled water I use at home, but without me asking, they add a loving scoop of sugar that honestly is heaven in a glass.

The first restaurant served a hibiscus sweet tea. It was absolute yum and had the prettiest color. The next was crushed ice and brown. I was not thinking about the calories. I told them to leave the pitcher. In heaven, I am going to hope for a spigot of this very thing. I drink lots and lots of tea, but honestly sweet tea is something special. It is satisfying. It was the star at our little table. The food took second place because the tea was so tasty.

Joy should be a current that flows in our lives. Alongside the most painful moments, hardest relationships, and greatest loss, joy can coincide. Happiness begins and ends with circumstance, but joy can exist in suffering. And because joy is holy, it can escape and operate outside of our present pain. You see, beloved, He doesn't just ask us to rejoice. He promises to bring us joy.

At this moment, perhaps joy feels foreign or even a false promise of God. Maybe your sadness, grief, or shame have filled the space that joy once had. Or possibly you have never known joy. Yet we see in His Word, joy is not just a hope. It is a promise. The prophet Isaiah tells us it is at the end of ourselves when He begins. He comes to "give unto them beauty for ashes, the oil of joy for mourning, the garment of praise for the spirit of heaviness; that they might be called trees of righteousness, the planting of the LORD, that he might be glorified" (Isaiah 61:3).

It is possible we are looking within for this joy and not without. If we add up our circumstances, it may not equal joy in the Webster-defined feeling of happiness. However, if we lay the wise words of Piper that the feeling of joy is in the soul and add the promises of Isaiah, joy takes on a much deeper and attainable definition. We are not the creators and curators of joy. He is.

He is in the business of beauty for ashes and praise from petition. Joy cannot and will not be a product of circumstance. Rejoicing is not a reaction to our circumstances. It is so much bigger. Joy is found in the soul where the Holy Spirit dwells. The Holy Spirit holds the transformational power cited in Romans, "Do not conform any longer to the pattern of this world, but be transformed by the renewing of your mind … Be joyful in hope, patient in affliction, faithful in prayer" (Romans 12:2, 12).

If you are lacking joy, dear one, submit the lack to Him and let Him love you through it. Although He certainly can and does change circumstances, the product of transformation is more often a heart change. It is the power of the Holy Spirit giving us fresh eyes, soft hearts, and renewed peace.

When we endeavor to find Him in His word, when we experience His presence and see His amazing power at work in ways we cannot understand, we can rejoice in the knowledge that fierce is not a product of us. It is a gift from Him.

He listens, and in the hardest of hard, we can have peace. We won't understand, but that's okay because He holds and guards our hearts and minds in the process. We can turn our thoughts from our troubles because He is thinking about those. We can turn to what He asks us to think about, those facets that are "true, noble, right, pure, lovely and admirable" (Philippians 4:8).

I once had a little girl in kindergarten Sunday school answer it this way. Teaching about Old Testament miracles, I asked the class what a "miracle" is. My little student responded, "It is God's kind of magic."

Our reaction, our choice, and our ability to rejoice is nothing short of miraculous. It is the knowing that He is there. He is in control. He sees the suffering and pain. Through the most amazing sense of what our souls need, He is working them for our good.

> Not only so, but we also glory in our sufferings, because we know that suffering produces perseverance; perseverance, character; and character, hope. And hope does not put us to shame, because God's love has been poured out into our hearts through the Holy Spirit, who has been given. (Romans 5:3–5)

8

Your Calling

Beloved, you are out walking on the ice. You are becoming fierce. Congratulations! You have stepped out knowing His **F**oundation is sure. You have **I**nvited Him in to all the spaces, including the ones you don't understand or weren't particularly proud of, the ones hidden and the ones in the light. You have surrendered in the holiest of ways to a God who carries our grief, bears our burdens, and comes alongside our sorrows. You have **E**xperienced His presence. He has left the church building where you were used to meeting Him, and He has become your constant companion. You have felt the Spirit of the living God as He inhabits you, you **R**ejoice in His companionship, and He reveals Himself more and more in scripture and your surroundings.

In this last year, a dear friend of mine received a new part to make her heart work well. The grandson of a beloved friend received a new heart. And my youngest daughter spent almost seven hours in the operating room as they took bone from her hip to build her upper gumline and cartilage from behind her ear to build an eardrum. Newness placed in oldness creates strength. That is the message of inviting and experiencing Jesus's presence, and this amazing transaction is something to rejoice in.

Rejoice is the verb of proclaiming, professing, and projecting joy. It is the joy that comes from a loving Father holding us when we are happy and when our hearts have shattered. It is the joy that comes from knowing He knows, cares, loves, and shelters. The joy that stretches before us gives us glimpses of eternity.

Now we take what we have learned, these four stops on our path to fierce, and we apply them to the last two, **C**alling and the **E**nlarging of our territory.

Almost every week, I get to have coffee with the teens at church. This last summer, the lovely girls and I read and studied a book together. The prior fall, their beloved Sunday school leaders retired, and I became their fill-in. In truth, after one summer of these people, I was smitten. The youth of today is not lost; they are finding. They are finding different solutions than some may like, but they are pelted with tons of information, which leads them to different destinations. We, the elder statesmen, can listen, applaud, point, and posture. It is important and worthwhile work. It is eye-opening and encouraging. Their wonder and wisdom give me courage.

Since I lack most of the answers to most of their questions, I come armed with questions. If you are wanting to share Jesus, ask questions. People love to talk about themselves. And as Bob Goff said, "Acceptance is better than information" (*A Flood of Love*). Asking questions invites people; it welcomes them. It provides the hospitality of a safe space and opens windows to their souls.

One of my early Sunday mornings with this lovely group, I asked, "If you could ask one question of God and get an answer today, what would it be?" The questions were epic, but one caught me because I have said it, the ladies in my women's group have studied it, and the teens queried the exact same question.

This sweet gal looked over her latte and said, "I want Him to tell me: what is my calling?"

This question has a kissing cousin, "Why am I here?"

Perhaps you have wondered that too. The former is the Christian version of the latter secular question. This is a deep and, quite literally, a soul-searching question. It is a question virtually all humans will wonder or ask. It is built in our DNA.

I have never studied psychology, but for about ten minutes in my college marketing class, we touched on something that frames this question, Maslow's hierarchy of needs. Maslow drew a pyramid that points and guides us through our needs; therefore our motivations emerge from the most basic physiological needs to the psychological needs that develop with age. First of course, as a child is formed in its mother's womb and for every day after, they will require food and water. In developed countries, we rarely ponder this event, yet we know we would go to great lengths in the absence of food or water to provide them for ourselves and our families. This need motivates us to work, plant, cook, and show up wherever we might need to be to access food and/or water.

Second, we want to feel safe. We mortgage our finances such that we will have a safe place to live where we can lock doors and darken windows and our children can play in safe backyards. Third, we are motivated by the love Christ has for us to find love in this life. Children are born as babies to see the modeling of love that their parents give them. This parental love models the love our heavenly Father has for us. Christian or non-Christian, in most cultures and apart from situations of abuse and addiction, a child soon learns that love is good. They hunger for it as much as a parent longs to give it. One of the many catastrophic events that occur through abuse or neglect is the breaking of this beautiful link from parental love and safeguarding to heavenly shelter.

The fourth of five needs is the need for accomplishment. That is, we need to belong, to have purpose, and to be a part of something bigger than ourselves. The fifth need expounds on the same theme. It is the need for self-actualization. We push to succeed in our work, strive for good grades, and put in overtime for promotions. We continually seek for the thing that God made us for and desperately want to know, our calling.

I find it wildly creative that every person's DNA varies. We are flesh and blood, bone and sinew. We may all possess two eyes, one nose, and one mouth, but we are not the same. I have a virtually identical upbringing to my brother, yet he runs a small farm, and I love to spend weekends in the city. God could have chosen all of us to have the same physical characteristics, and yet we are as varied as wildflowers. He could have given us similar passions, yet no one, even the most dedicated, bear the exact same perspectives as someone else. When He talks about the body of Christ, He quite literally means some carry or walk us forward, see the future, hear the present, taste the wonder, hold the suffering, cook the meals, or clean the dishes. All are vitally, wonderfully, miraculously important, and impeccably different.

Paul wrote about the artistic God who sees in us the bearers of His truth, "For we are God's masterpiece, (workmanship, handiwork) created in Christ Jesus to do good works, which God prepared in advance for us" (Ephesians 2:10). It is critically important that we understand we serve a loving, giving, compassionate God who is not hiding our purpose. In the psalms, He writes our job description,

> Better is one day in your courts than a thousand elsewhere; I would rather be a doorkeeper in the house of my God than dwell in the tents of the wicked. For the Lord God is a sun and shield; the Lord bestows favor and honor; no good thing does He withhold from those whose walk is blameless. (Psalm 84:10–11)

We are here, dear one, to know Him and let Him be known. Period. The end. This is why He lends us breath, to know Him and to tell our neighbors and new acquaintances who He is. Within the framework of that calling lies our professions, our passions, and our pursuits. Paul puts it this way,

> I urge you to live a life worthy of the calling you have received. Be completely humble and gentle, be patient, bearing one another in love. Make every effort to keep the unity of the Spirit through the bond of peace. There is one body and one Spirit-just as you were called to one hope when you were called- one Lord, one faith, one baptism; one God and Father of all, who is over all and through all and in all. It was He who gave some to be apostles, some to be prophets, some to be evangelists, and some to be pastors and teachers, to prepare God's people for the works of service, so that the body of Christ may be built up. (Ephesians 4:1–6, 11–12)

From Ephesus to your living room, we get to know Him. We study His Word, invite Him in, and experience the presence of His Spirit, and then we embrace His calling on our lives. The purpose, passion, and calling, the entire mélange, seems similar, and yet they are distinct and different.

Our purpose is to know Him and let Him be known. Jeremiah

Johnston says it this way in *Unanswered*, "The ultimate purpose of life is not our happiness but rather the knowledge of God derived through a relationship with Jesus Christ." We take that knowledge and find a way to share it. That is living life on and with purpose.

Our passion wakes us and keeps us up at night. It is the thing we want to make right, the problem we want to solve, or the group we want to help. It is the thing that happened to us that we want to prevent from happening to anyone else. It is the piercing arrow from the Holy Spirit for which our heart bleeds.

Our calling is the piece of this passion. For a passion to be a calling, it must bear spiritual fruit, but I am moving too quickly past passion. Let's explore this. Let's find yours. Let's put a few of the puzzle pieces together to see the wild beauty you are.

It might feel scattered or confused. It might seem overwhelming and hard. You might decide you are too old or the bank account too small to pursue your calling, but let's stay together as we ask some questions remembering my role and yours are the same. We are to know Him and let Him be known.

I am quite certain, however, that your venue looks different than mine. Your visitors are people I may never meet. Your gift to them is a talent or technique that I do not possess. Your words, language, style, and grace are all genuinely and grace-given to fill the space you have been given.

I am going to weave lots of questions here. I hope you will take a pencil in your hand and write down your answers and thoughts to truly firm up the thoughts in your mind. Write down what first comes to your mind. I am a big fan of notebooks. Journaling would be too fancy of a word, but I keep notebooks handy to write lists, quotes, and things that stir me. In the back of this book, you will find prompts. Fierce steps may require some remembrance and reflection.

Please know that not every question will resonate. The formula is not the same for everyone. The Holy Spirit gives you His heart language. For me, it might be a whisper. In you, perhaps it's a voice. In others, possibly it is a vision or confidence in knowing or understanding something that you have only thought of before.

Let's start simply. (These questions are also in the Footsteps section at the back of the book in order, and remember, I am praying for you as you ponder!)

What are you passionate about? Maybe you are passionate about food or human trafficking. Don't judge your thoughts. We need everyone at this party, or we would be bored to tears. If you can, challenge yourself to name more than one thing. Let your mind run. Were you passionate about something as a teen or when you watch the news? Does something keep you up at night and wake you in the morning?

Perhaps naming your passions is simple, or maybe you are staring at the page, wanting to close this book. Stay for a while. Let's imagine I have brewed a hot pot of tea or a lovely carafe of coffee. We use real cream at my house, and because I love us, there are cookies out between us because this is important work and we need nourishment.

Listing not to your liking? Let's try something else. Think back to before you were ten years old. Was there something you loved to do? Think of something you did with your mom or dad. It was the thing you truly enjoyed and the activity your parents applauded. It was your time with them or your moment to shine. Think of the thing that you and your friend did, the one activity that made you feel so special because you both had this one interest. Write it down.

Or perhaps in junior high or high school you truly loved participating in a sport or hobby, learning a certain language, or going on a mission trip. Jot it down. When you were in college or a young adult, you dreamed about doing this one thing, but the practicality of finances and time or the fear of failure deflated the dream. Write it down. Your passion may be tucked under things and hidden in parts of your heart where you rarely go.

Your questions will read like this: What do I fear most? If I had three months to live, what would I do? For example, if I had to answer this question today, I would go to the Congo. My husband and I have befriended a pastor there. The pictures and songs that Brother Jessie has sent of his school and church have caused me to long for people I have never met. Their prayers in French go on for hours. Their songs are filled with joy in spaces that have no running water and limited access to food. I want to understand this and be a part of this. We are passionate about this. If I had three months to live, I would pack my husband and my children and go to the Congo.

Last but certainly not least, ask this question: if money or time were not obstacles, what would I do? Let us reach beyond what we have to what God can do. "You do not have, because you do not ask" (James 4:2b). Let your mind dream, and let God build. God is talking, dear one. Listen.

We should spend as much time listening to God as we do talking. The listening and waiting takes incredible discipline, but He is faithful to communicate to our hearts and ears. Open yourself up to Him. He is present in His word. He is present through the Holy Spirit, and He will testify to your passion through the testimony of brothers and sisters in Christ. Your passion is the birthplace of your calling. It is the spark that lights the fire of your calling.

In the words of Frederick Buechner, "The place where God calls you to is the place where your deep gladness and the world's deep hunger coincide"(6). It is a holy place. Your calling may be part time, full time, or some time. Dr. Clyde Narramore wrote, "Your natural abilities are God's suggestions for your life's work" (*Women's Devotional Bible*, 36)

Don't get scared at the phrase "life's work." Perhaps you are already saying that this won't work. Maybe your position as a cashier at the grocery doesn't mirror the passion in your heart. Hallelujah, dear one! You are providing a home, food, and rest for you and your family. That does not negate your calling. It is part of the equation. Your calling is unique. It is designed exclusively for you and has been built for you. Think of the crazy thing you liked as a kid. Don't believe everyone can do it. It is yours from Him. The talent, time, or temperament your calling requires, He has woven that together to give you a glimpse of "a life worthy of your calling" (Philippians 1:27–30).

Your stage might be your backyard or a foreign country. You may put your monies and time into saving human lives or growing flowers to deliver to shut-ins. You may make the best bean salsa in the world and bring it (with chips) to people (or me) in your church to fellowship and be Jesus at their kitchen table. Thank you, Patty. Your job may be secular or sacred. Your calling is the intersection of your hand with your heart.

Have you studied your enneagram? Perhaps you still question how you and your calling equate to more than two. Take this test. Dive into the divine personality God has directed you to be. The helpers help. The leaders lead. The individualist does all sorts of cool stuff and copies no one.

Some of us make peace; others reform. To do all God has for us, we must find our passion and listen to our call. It is an extraordinary thing to be in God's will. If you are hungering and thirsting for Him and if you are reflecting His glory on your sidewalk or in your boardroom, you, beloved, are in His will.

You see it is not the who. We know and love Him. We want everyone to hear His words, feel His love, and understand His compassion. It is not the what either. We know the what. You may be a great singer, painter, babysitter, or cabinet organizer. They won't remember the note you sang or the can you alphabetized. They will remember how they felt being in your presence because they were in the presence of the Spirit that dwells within you.

The when is now. I have heard so many people say when: when I am older, when I am thinner, when I retire, when I feel better, when my kids grow up, and so forth. There is never a season we cannot serve the King because there is never a moment where His Spirit is not willing or working or incredibly wonderful. The where is the wonder.

As I write these thoughts, my oldest son is in graduate school. He moved east almost exactly a year ago. I watched as the truck loaded up, and all I could think about is the little trucks we played with for hours and hours when he was a wee boy. He was my first, and for six years, he was the only one. We had a little blue suitcase filled with little trucks. Those trucks went everywhere with us. On trash day, the trash truck would sit on the windowsill, and the candy truck would deliver candy to the trash man. I don't remember having a moving truck until that day in August. It was a hard day.

To say the transition has been difficult would be an understatement. The East Coast is not the Midwest. Folks are not as forgiving, and big state universities don't provide the prayer covering of small Christian colleges. He has precious friends there. He has great work and good teaching. But whenever he calls and I am cooking, he asks, "Will you cook that when I am home?" And whenever I tell him where I am, he will say, "I wish I were there."

The difficulty in the calling is not the calling. It is not knowing the where. It is not being sure of the city, job, school, or street. Like my son being far from home, we must understand that we are not home and we will be homesick this side of heaven. The discontent is the disconnect from the spiritual home He intended. We were not supposed to live in sin sickness, to be separated, or to wonder. We were supposed to walk with Him.

The hole you feel is not the lack of calling; it is the lack your created being feels being separate from the presence of our Creator. The devil crawled in, quite literally, and tried to steal our souls away. He started a war that is still fought every day of every single year in each mind and heart for every moment until we meet Jesus. We need to be battle-ready. If this feels hard and exhausting, it is. It is the relentless fight to keep the enemy out of our thoughts, homes, work, passion, and personalities. The devil is far more present than we care to admit or acknowledge.

A battle is waging. It is a battle for our minds and hearts, and the devil would delight in detouring us from our destination to fierce and our destination home to heaven. As I have prayed for you, I found the battle is most significant when we are trying to define our next steps, that is, our passion and ability to walk to fierce. We must stop here for just a moment and discuss this battle. Ignorance is not bliss, and the enemy is very real.

To understand this battle, we must define who He is and who we are. And we must with everything in us be battle-ready. The word gives the enemy one purpose and many names. John 10:10 says, "The thief comes ONLY to STEAL and KILL and DESTROY, I (JESUS) have come that you may have life and have it to the full" (emphasis added).

I have heard demons speak. I have heard them speak in prayer for a dear sister oppressed with demons. There is nothing subtle or soft about them. They and the devil are on one singular mission, to kill. They steal our peace of mind; they destroy the sanctity, hope, and love of believers. They attempt to kill us both physically and spiritually. They can destroy our hope of heaven, image of Jesus, and knowledge that we are His children and His dearly loved. If they can so confuse our call and purpose, if they can establish our unworthiness when Christ Himself has made us worthy, they have won.

Open the book of Ephesians. It is a short book, six chapters that will introduce you to who you are. Further, no war is fought without a strategy. Ephesians draws up the battle plan and dresses us for it as well. Ephesians 1: 3–7 takes a long stroll through who you are in Jesus:

- We are BLESSED with every spiritual blessing in Christ, not one or two, but EVERY. If the devil tells you that you are lacking, whisper this one. It works.
- We are CHOSEN. You are no accident, afterthought, or mistake. You are chosen. Why? "To be HOLY and BLAMELESS in his sight" (Ephesians 1:4).
- We are ADOPTED, "as his sons (and daughters) in accordance with his PLEASURE and will" (Ephesians 1:5). No matter what family means to you, realize you are His. He desperately wants you, not as a friend but as a child. You are loved, cared for, and sought after by a heavenly parent.
- We are REDEEMED. Oh, beloved, do not carry shame. Take it to Jesus. Do not own the sins you have given Him. He has forgotten them. Do not listen to the whispers that you are not good enough, pretty enough, or smart enough. And do not ever believe that He does not know what you have done. He does. He is and has redeemed you.

"Having believed you were marked in Him with a seal, the promised Holy Spirit, who is a deposit GUARANTEEING our inheritance until the redemption of those who are God's possession—to the praise of His glory" (Ephesians 1:13–14, emphasis added).

Perhaps you have never read, embraced, or believed this before. Maybe you struggle in opening up the Word. Stay with me and read on to Ephesians 1:17–20. Paul gets it; he knows it is hard. He tells us and the church at Ephesus,

> I keep asking that the God of our Lord Jesus Christ, the glorious Father, may give you the Spirit of wisdom and revelation, so that you MAY KNOW HIM BETTER. I pray also that the eyes of your heart may be enlightened in order that you may know the HOPE to which HE HAS CALLED YOU, the riches of his glorious inheritance in the saints, and his incomparably great power for us who believe. (emphasis added).

I hope you don't think I am shouting. When my youngest daughter leaves a note in my briefcase, she writes in all capital letters. She tells me to have a GREAT day and remember the ROSES and not the thorns. She doesn't write in the lines. She doesn't need them. I like that Ava Joy lives life big and to the fullest; we should too. Let's capitalize on the power God has given us. He wants us too. He wants us to live free, to be surrendered, and to embrace the grace He has given us and the love He has for us. Let us pray daily as Paul did for ourselves and each other. Ephesians 3:16–19 reads,

> I pray that out of his glorious riches he may strengthen you with power through His Spirit in your inner being, so that Christ may dwell in your hearts through faith. And I pray that you, being ROOTED and ESTABLISHED IN LOVE, may have POWER, together with all the saints, to grasp HOW WIDE AND LONG AND HIGHT AND DEEP IS THE LOVE OF CHRIST AND TO KNOW THIS LOVE THAT SURPASSES KNOWLEDGE— THAT YOU MAY BE FILLED TO THE MEASURE OF ALL THE FULLNESS OF GOD. (emphasis added)

This is our part right now, wherever you are reading to say, shout, and sing, "Hallelujah!"

The battles are already won. This is hope. This is it. This is promise. This is the created God saying to you, not you but we, that you and He can do this. We can live this life, stand strong on His foundation, invite His Spirit, and experience His presence, love, grace, and mercy so we will not only be battle-ready but also rejoice in Him and our salvation.

For one quick second, we get it, and then the very next, the enemy is trying to steal it away. This is not by accident, and it is not out of your fear, shame, or guilt. This is what he does. Remember earlier in Chapter 2, we learned, "If it is not a thought you would wish for yourself, it is probably the enemy."

Sit there for just a bit. Think for just a moment about one negative thought you have. Perhaps the thought deals with your appearance or intelligence. Maybe the enemy likes to mention your past or failed performance. You could wish all day you could shut him up, but we cannot in our strength. But we know who can, and the unbelievable and miraculous truth is, it is the One that lives in you.

He waits for you. He asks you to knock on the door. He is exactly and incredibly there, waiting outside. The sin you feel, confess it and invite the God of the universe to dwell in your heart. The devil has this uncanny way of personalizing every story. He tells us we are failures or foreigners to the kingdom when we, beloved, are in fact residents of the kingdom of heaven. The devil wants us to believe our problem is our neighbor, spouse, coworker, or the abuse we suffered as children. The battle, the struggle, is far bigger than the one in our mind. It is fought on the spiritual battlefield with a legion of angels at our side. Ephesians 6:12 puts it this way, "Our struggle is not against flesh and blood, but against the rulers, against the authorities, against the powers of this dark world and against the spiritual forces of evil in the heavenly realms."

Take the hurt you have nursed and give it to Him. Take the lie that you are not enough and stand on the fact that He is. Take the shame you have buried and invite Him in. He loves you, and He already knew. Share it with Him and know He throws it in a sea of forgetfulness, never to be brought up by Him again.

He mentions us, His children, again and again in the Word. But always remember the story is really His. We find Him as well as His power and might, and it causes us to know we can be bravely fierce.

Are we battle-ready? Let's get dressed. I wonder from time to time if on any given day I spend as much time with Jesus as I do in front of my mirror or inside my closet. I shower in the evening and getting ready for work in the morning is almost a science. If I have given any thought to clothes the night before, which quite frankly is a big if, I can be out the door in twenty minutes. Do I share twenty minutes with Him first thing in the morning? Do I share my thoughts, invite Him in, or give Him my day? This, dear one, is the essence of a relationship with Him. This is prayer. C. S. Lewis wrote, "I pray because I can't help myself. I pray because I am helpless. I pray because the need flows out of me all the time—waking and sleeping. It doesn't change God—it changes me."

We must change the way we think, to know God is in us and with us, fighting this battle. We must embrace freedom; we must pray. Prayer is an ongoing verbal and nonverbal conversation with our Father. He desperately wants you and me to know He is present and sovereign. He is all-knowing and all-powerful. It is worship and wonder all in one breath.

Paul admonishes us in Ephesians 6:10 to be strong. Strength begins in prayer. Prayer has to be the underbelly and covering of everything we do. When Paul penned these words, He was sitting in prison. My dear friend and pastor, Kurt, spent some part of the last few months teaching on this handful of verses, the armor of God (Ephesians 6:12–18). I had read these verses and even taught on them, but never did it occur to me that from a prison cell, Paul was looking at a Roman guard. He would have been seeing someone in armor.

God used what had to be a horrible set of circumstances for His glory. He knew for thousands of years until He returns that His children would need this representation to be battle-ready. He set a guard in armor outside that prison door so Paul could paint this picture. It is both figurative and formative. If we visit this daily, as we ready ourselves for our day, we must remember we ready ourselves for much more.

> Put on the full armor of God so that you can take your stand against the devil's schemes. For our struggle is NOT against flesh and blood, but against the rulers, against the authorities, against the powers of this dark world and against the evil in the heavenly realms. Therefore, put on the full armor of God, so that when the day of evil comes, you may be able to stand your ground, and after you have done everything to stand. Stand firm then. (Ephesians 6:10–14a)

And then, beloved, He gives us a picture of our armor. Six critical pieces are put together, all strategically placed to cover the body and secure the soul. Each one is necessary, essential, and carefully appointed for protection, posture, and position.

We start with truth. A belt will hold both our breastplate and secure our weapon. In the truth and foundation, we know at least a handful of the seven thousand promises in the Word. Recite them, know them, and say them out loud when the devil whispers, and he has to flee. He cannot stand in the presence of the Holy Word.

Then we secure our breastplate. It covers our heart and secures our spirit. The knowledge that we are made right in Him is an incredible gift and encouragement to every person who has said, thought, and done evil. He forgives and wants us to live forgiven.

I don't know about you, but I am not a runner. I have tried hard. I know it is great for me and frees me from the pain of arthritis on the rare mornings I can convince myself I can do it. But sorry, Bruce Springsteen, this baby girl was not born to run. I cannot outrun anyone, especially the devil. He inhabits my home, work, mind, and even church.

I have to be ready to overtake him with peace. There is no accident here. We are to wear the shoes of peace such that we can walk in peace, but not world peace or green peace, the peace that can only come from the Father of peace that encourages and admonishes us that He is all good. And in that simple fact, we can have peace.

Ephesians 6:16 reads that the shield for this soldier of Rome was huge. Four feet in height, it would cover the body and provide protection for whatever the enemy was throwing or shooting at the shoulder. Flaming arrows? What are yours? Mine are many: fear for my children, discouragement for my business, friends falling away from faith, or a world that has lost its focus on good and decency and has traded it for an assembly of evil and selfishness.

The shield is that of faith—that is, the faith in Him, the faith that even the smallest faith that can, as Matthew writes, move mountains. He sees and knows this mustard seed of faith and is willing to plant it in His almighty garden such that the thing that seems so very large to us, the mountain, will move. It has little to do with our little faith; it has everything to do with a mighty God. He takes delight in proving Himself faithful.

He lines the path up to His will and sets the direction with heaven in mind and the thing for which we prayed is answered according to our greatest good. I am so very grateful He has not always answered prayers the way I have asked or demanded.

I have told Him how things should run, how they should finish, and how they would best look. I have brought Him in after I have made plans and crossed off hundreds of items on dozens of lists. But always, even when I couldn't see His hand because mine were blocking His, He has proved Himself faithful, good, and wonderful.

I told him in January sixteen years ago that I was ready to head to Kazakhstan. On January 13, we were given the most precious picture of a little girl that we hoped would become our daughter. Days later, we were given one week to prep, and I had packed a thousand things. I had thought of a hundred ways to make sure we abided by the weight limit and had everything our new little daughter and our two- and eight-year-old boys would need. My heart was so ready, but then our agency said another week and then another and another.

It was week five. I was alone in the house. Brian had taken the boys, and I began to pray and then cry and yell. I had organized every piece of clothing down to the day. I had ziplocked every gift we needed for the orphanage workers. I had the nursery ready, clothes bought, and every agenda item crossed off for my office in my absence. Only we were not getting clearance to go. It felt scary and wrong. We had come so far, only to hit a full dead stop. I prayed for her, but anger rose up in me at the situation and God. How could He guide us this far to then fall silent? I told Him how unfair it was that I was missing these weeks with my daughter. I told Him how desperate I was to hold her and stamp every piece of paper to make her mine.

I was angrier with God than at any other moment of my life. He felt capricious and foreign. Every step had been so orchestrated and ordained. I felt Him. I prepared with Him, not without, and now I felt unequivocally alone.

In two weeks, along with my lists and my Ziploc bags, my boys and my husband boarded a plane. Five weeks later, we sat with our daughter and the orphanage director saying our goodbyes and expressing our gratitude. He cautioned us to take care of her well and mentioned her terrible bout with bronchitis before our arrival. He casually mentioned her weeks in the hospital in late January, and then through our Russian translator, he said, "Had you come any sooner, you would not have been eligible to adopt Lily because her health was so frail."

I froze in the fragility of it all. My requests and my demands, clothed in my plans and agenda, had almost undone His best. Even when we cannot see, His eyes are on us. Even when we cannot understand, His wisdom is writing our story. And when we are at the end, relying on our last nerve, it is there He gives us a peek at His glory.

The last parts of the armor, one worn and one held, bear incredible power and significance. The helmet protects the head and of course symbolizes salvation. The Savior has come. We can read the end of the book, and that end changes everything. We may suffer pain and loss. We may endure depression and desolation. We may have lived decades in sin led by selfish ambition, but the moment you throw up your hands in surrender and relinquish your hearts to the Savior, you, beloved, have a room ready in heaven.

This is a game-changer. The thoughts will come into your mind as they have ten thousand times before, but this time and every next moment, you can remind the thief that there is a new sheriff in town. And His name is Jesus. His name, His Word, and His authority have been given to us, and with it, every single demon must flee.

Paul prayed, and I intercede with these words for you right at this moment, "I pray also that the eyes of your heart may be enlightened in order that you may know the hope to which he has called you, the riches of his glorious inheritance in the saints, and his incomparably great power for us who believe" (Ephesians 1:18–19).

Prayer, although not a physical piece of armor, is often referred to as the seventh piece of armor. Prayer deserves its own number and its own place in our hearts, days, and lives. Prayer is not only a piece of armor that protects; it plays the dual role of weapon. Martin Luther said, "To be a Christian without prayer is not more possible than to be alive without breathing" (Wiersby, 152).

I wonder where and when you pray. Do you have a prayer closet or a war room? Do you pray when you get up or only when you lie down? Do you pray at the side of your bed, or is prayer a language for you? Is it one that you speak throughout the day in quiet whispers and spoken thoughts? Are you waiting for answers even now? Do you have a pattern when you pray: thankfulness first, requests second, and perhaps listening third? Are you a prayer walker? Did you notice in the Word that this is the one thing the disciples were perhaps the most curious about? They specifically—and I think strategically—asked Jesus to "teach us to pray" (Luke 11:1).

Don't you love that? They could have asked to learn a million things from the omniscient, omnibenevolent, omnipotent friend, yet it was prayer. It's the thirst for knowledge perhaps, but I believe with all my heart the dozen witnessed the cadence of Jesus's prayer life, the retreating to speak to His Father, the peace that no doubt followed Him after prayer, the assurance that what He said was heard, our words whispered into heaven, and His answers whispered into our hearts.

The disciples craved the secret of a contented life. So do we. And that secret is prayer. It is the knowledge that no thought is too simple, no emotion too raw, no need too great, and no situation too grave. He listens. We are heard. As C. S. Lewis wrote, "I pray because I am helpless. I pray because the need flows out of me all the time—waking and sleeping. It doesn't change God—it changes me."

I wonder if this is the essence of what Paul wrote in Romans when he talked about the transforming nature of the Holy Spirit. He begins, "Do not copy or conform any longer to the pattern of the world" (Romans 12:2a).

I am going to pause there. What is the pattern of the world? We have sin first and foremost, so clearly that is a pattern. We, the children of Israel, every generation on every continent, have and will fall short of the glory of God. But when I think pattern, I think how we are cut. The pattern is the paper laying on the fabric. Do we look, act, and behave like everyone else? Are we anxious, worried, and striving with an insatiable thirst for more time, talent, or treasure?

Paul wrote to the church at Thessalonica with the command to "be joyful, PRAY CONTINUALLY, give thanks in all circumstances, for this is God's will for you in Jesus Christ." Let's travel back to Romans 12:2b. We are not to copy the world, not to conform to its pattern, "BUT be TRANSFORMED by the renewing of your mind." This renewal, this transformation, and this rising out of the angst and anger of this world is only possible with an attitude of prayer, a constant continual conversation with our Father.

In addressing the Passion Conference, Louie Giglio said one of the greatest truths about prayer I have ever heard, "If we could see what happens when we pray we would never cease to pray" ("Never Cease to Pray"). We can only hope to take on His nature, to understand His ways, to feel His love, to grasp His mercy, and to hold His grace when we talk and listen to Him.

Prayer is not subject to place or posture. It is the ongoing conversation of two beings getting to know, love, and trust one another. It offers the transcendence of earthly space to the glory of heaven. He refreshes the weary and calms the worry all by the act of prayer. Stormie Omartian uses the words "specific" and "strategic." I believe wholeheartedly that we must, in order to survive this planet earth, be both specific and strategic in prayer. We fight a war. What words could suggest a battle plan more than "specific" and "strategic"? And let me add one more: prayer must also be ceaseless.

Let me explain. We must dedicate a time and place in our day in which we can lay our people and problems before God. It is not only an act of obedience but an offensive posture of foregoing control. It is giving Him our people and problems with the permission to do in and with them what only He can do.

For some, writing prayers is key; for others, it is speaking them out loud. For others, myself included, I walk out my prayers. Early in the morning, I go outside and pray. There is something about a starry sky or a sunrise, rain, and snow that remind me of the bigness of God. I never tire of remembering how great He is, and in every quantifiable sense, it dwarfs my burdens. Not that I or even He thinks they are small, but in His hands, they seem so much more manageable.

On one street, I pray for my pastor and His family. I pray for my family and children. On another street, I list those I know who do not know Him. I pray for wisdom when and if I get to speak to them, and I pray for the Holy Spirit to intersect with their lives in ways I cannot see or simulate.

I pray for the events of my day and ongoing needs, some medical, material, or mundane. I thank Him probably further to the end of my prayers than polite, but He listens, hears, answers, and seems unendingly patient with a Midwest girl who asks too much. I listen too. I wish I could tell you I listen as much as I talk, but in these kinds of books, lying is frowned upon. But I am learning. I am learning to listen for Him, the heart language that comes from an attentive spirit, the one that brings faces to mind and scripture to remembrance and peace in pain. He is so faithful, and truly I do not want to miss one moment with Him.

Prayer, specific and strategic, is all this and more. Prayer can and should be ceaseless. I cannot show love to my husband or children without communication. I cannot get to know friends or strangers without speaking. Throughout the day, I am in almost a constant conversation with Him. It is a soul speak. It is inviting Him into the hard spaces of heartache and the joyful spaces of the perfect gift found in the aisle at Salvation Army. It is the knowledge and trust that He is always there, always available to share and author the monotonous and miraculous. There are so many lonely hearts in the world. He is the friend of the forsaken. His presence is the very essence of light in the darkness. If you don't believe me, invite Him. Turn on some worship music, speak your heart out to Him, and notice how the room of the mind changes. Find calm and curiosity where anxiety and angst once lived. It is extraordinary.

Some who are reading this have unanswered prayers, perhaps boatloads of them. I stand with you, and I hope you know I am hugging you in prayer just now. His will is often easier to understand than His way. His way, in some circumstances and souls, may only be revealed on the other side of heaven. The Holy Spirit is at work answering prayers and preparing hearts every moment of every day. He intercedes on our behalf for our good. We must trust when we cannot see this holy work, and this trust is the absolute essence of faith. "Now faith is the substance of things hoped for, the evidence of things not seen" (Hebrews 11:1).

Praying and waiting for answers are two parts of a very holy trinity. The third piece is fasting. I was well into my forties before I understood the gift of fasting. For years, I would hear the word, and my mind would travel to forty days in the desert. Forty days in the desert, strike one. No water, strike two. And no food? I am headed back to the dugout. Fortunately, neither my pastors nor the Holy Spirit let me stay in my stubborn seat of judgment. There are some prayers so big and many problems so perplexing that we must consider fasting to hear and see God. This sounds so incredibly spiritual, and on one hand, it is, but on the other, it is absolutely practical. Removing something from our day or diet opens up white space. There is both an element of calendar and character here. I would be so bold as to say that fierceness will become dependent on fasting. It is a spiritual connection out of a sacrificial act.

> When you fast, put oil on your head and wash your face, so that it will not be obvious to men that you are fasting, but only to your Father who is unseen; and your

Father, who sees what is done in secret, **will reward you**. (Matthew 6:17–18, emphasis added)

I don't understand the math of this. I don't in any way believe that prayers with fasting are answered faster than prayers without; rather the lack of something, whether food or pleasure, opens the eyes and ears to another kind of seeing and listening. One becomes so in tune to the subject of the fast that the melody of the answers is louder and clearer than any prayer ever prayed. I can testify to the abundance of scarcity. I rarely have mustered the discipline to fast all day. For me, it has been a series of lunches or dinners. For me, it has been directed at a certain unanswered heartache. I measure a space in time and withdraw a meal, practice, or pleasure, and He fills that space with His presence. The hunger is a reminder, the change in pattern, a unique place that He inhabits.

9

Enlarging Our Territory

Our Last Step to Fierce

Nestled in 1 Chronicles 4, God tucks in four short verses. He records the prayer of one of His own, Jabez. This simple prayer is a powerful guide and beautiful pattern of prayer for those seeking to be fierce.

> Jabez was more honorable than his brothers. His mother had named him Jabez, saying, "I gave birth to him in pain." Jabez cried out to the God of Israel, "Oh, that you would bless me and enlarge my territory! Let your hand be with me and keep me from harm so that I will be free from pain." And God granted his request. (1 Chronicles 4:9–10)

Before we unpack this prayer, let's take a moment and review where we have been to set the space for where we are going. I wonder as you stood on the edge of your pond: what did you see? Did you sense a firm foundation? Or do you now? Have you grabbed a handful of scriptures and pasted them on your mirror? Have they become new friends, or have you dusted off old promises that you knew as a child? Do you know that you know that He is sure and you as His child are entitled to all the seven thousand promises in His Word? He will not fail or forsake. He is our forever sure and solid foundation on which we can stand with the company of the saints.

Have you invited Him in? Do you sense His presence in the stillness and solitude of your mind? Have you allowed Him to open doors that have been sealed shut, stealing your peace and forbidding your forgiveness? Have you opened one or more? It is a daily moment-to-moment ritual. He knocks; we open again and again. Nothing is too ugly for Him to make beautiful, and nothing is too wrong for Him to make right. He knew your shame and guilt as He hung on the cross. The only one that remembers them is you, and He begs you to know the price was paid, the sin was forgiven, and the chain was absolutely and forever broken. We exchange our slavery to sin for a new master who has sanctified our souls.

Have you experienced His closeness? Do you sense His presence? As you opened His Word, have you asked Him to sit with you? Have you given Him space and time to answer? Perhaps it is your drive to work or some other menial task that has moved from mundane to ordained because it is your time with Him. You have come to welcome Him and to abandon your loneliness for loveliness. His Spirit soothes, gives us permission to surrender, and designs the desire of our hearts to love and serve, and in that ethereal expanse, we find with joy our calling.

Is there something holding you back? What is its name? Fear, shame, guilt, weight, health, or some perceived lack of skill or wisdom? Jabez, named for the birthing pains his mother endured, could have been named anything, and we would have moved forward without a thought of his situation. Yet don't we wonder if this name were a thorn to him? Was this the thing the children teased him about in school? Names, like words, have power.

We stand with Jabez. My life, his life, and your life are far from perfect. There is always something that keeps us where we are, short of where we think we should be, shy of the territory God has for us. Jabez was not content in this lack. He prayed for more. He asked for blessing, yes, blessing. This shows a child asking His dad to pour out what He has, knowing what he asks will be the right portion at the right time for the right motive to do the right thing. Scripture tells us Jabez "cried out to God." Jabez prayed and asked for three things. First, it was for blessing.

Do we struggle with this? I do. I will pray the stars and moon down on my family and friends, but for me? It's hard. Why? It sounds selfish and self-serving, yet every day of every month of every year, my children ask me for stuff, and according to what is healthy, edifying, and fulfilling for them, it is my absolute joy to give it to them. Why do we rob God of the same joy? Let us ask the Father to bless us because truly we "have not because we do not ask" (James 4:2b).

Second, Jabez says "enlarge my territory." I reconciled this for many years to mean Jabez was a farmer that simply wanted more land. With more land, he could feed his family and perhaps many others, but the Word does not say land. It is broader and wider than that. What is your territory? And in enlarging it, how could we let others know Him? Perhaps your territory reaches no farther than your front door. Maybe it's a few kids and a life. What would expansion look like?

Let's not frame this with things to do, but thoughts to have and ways God can open our minds, our hearts, and our hands. I remember those days well, thoughts of keeping and feeding our children well, teaching them right from wrong, and making sure they made it to the next grade, all while shepherding their spirits.

My eldest son was no more than five. A little boy the same age lived directly across the backyard. I delighted in the fact that we had a built-in playmate. At least socially, we seemed to be succeeding as parents.

We had a turtle-shaped sandbox. Every day Bailey and his buddy would find their way to the box and build and play. I visited in the yard with the other moms. I noticed the boys getting up and down, on the deck, and to the back door and back, but they were happy, laughing, and delighted. What could go wrong?

I returned to the house ready to start supper and asked Bailey what he was up to. "We had to bury a dead bug, Mama." He seemed determined. I reached the deck and then our screen door and noticed a very large pile of sand just inside the house. I was sure 90 percent of the turtle sandbox had been carefully shoveled into the house.

I turned and asked Bailey, "Where did you find the bug?"

He replied, "The screen door smooshed it!"

Naturally the place of the bug's passing was also the place of its burial. I didn't handle this well. I marched back over to the mom of our beloved playmate and explained the situation. She scolded her boy; I admonished mine. We jointly swept and shoveled pounds of sand back to its turtle home. Bailey was astonished at my anger. He felt he had done the respectful and kind thing to the injured insect.

I have told that story for years. It was the first time my tiny son had truly navigated to mischief. I have wondered often since then what God might have done with that moment, had I been listening or even trying to hear over my loud scolding and sweeping.

We cannot forgo our emotions, but God can and does change our attitudes. He will give us humor and insight. He will allow us to see our children and spouses, friends, and family the way He sees them. He will put our sand on the scale of importance and remind us that eternity matters.

Perhaps your territory is an office where the language does not honor God or the business of the day is the criticism of the person in the next cubicle. And maybe your Jabez is the fear of being unliked if you stand up or stay silent. What would expansion look like?

Our God is wildly creative. He opens hearts we cannot. He can bring circumstances in our lives or the lives of our coworkers where our very wide and differing opinions and beliefs can be bridged with a listening ear and calming voice. Yes, we stand in the gap to bring the gospel, but the gospel often starts with goodness, thoughtfulness, fairness, and loveliness. In a time when the world seems to be on fire with division and dissension, we must start here. We must always lead with the love of God.

Perhaps you are sitting alone with me looking for fierce, but life already seems too busy or hard, or you feel simply too tired. I have been there. Let's push open this door a little wider together. Maybe enlarging your territory feels like one more thing, but let's wonder for just a moment if it is not one more thing, but *the thing* about which you have dreamt, the thing you know He is leading you to, or the thing that keeps you up at night because the reality of day exposes the obstacles.

He knows this, dear one. Let us allow Him to take our thoughts captive. For just a moment, run wild with Him in the field of your mind. "We demolish arguments and every pretension that sets itself up against the knowledge of God, and we take captive every thought to make it obedient to Christ" (2 Corinthians 10:5).

He knows your budget and schedule. He knows the reasons why not. He will supply. "And my God will meet **all your needs** according to the riches of his glory in Christ Jesus" (Philippians 4:19, emphasis added). This is a promise of the time, money, wisdom, and will. It is the territory.

If we had no needs, if we had it all covered, or if there were no obstacles, we would simply not need Him. This gap from insufficiency to His sufficiency and from our lack to His abundance is the step to our new territory. Sometimes it is a new place, situation, relationship, and juxtaposition of what we have felt we **had** to do to what we **get** to do. The same job becomes a mission field. The same task becomes worship. And sometimes, a door opens to something wildly different.

Not too long ago, I was praying this Jabez prayer. Like Jabez, I wanted my territory enlarged. I felt God was leading us to adopt again. There was the stirring that somewhere there was more for us to do. And yes, every doubt that could be mustered appeared. Was it adoption? The thought brought the frustration of our age and the daunting task of the process. I have known this call two times before. It was sure and solid. This feeling didn't feel sure or solid, yet I knew He was speaking. I simply could not hear with discernment or decision. And in between every thought wedged the fear of Him asking more than I could give.

Jabez concludes His prayer with the words, "keep me from harm so that I will be free from pain" (1 Chronicles 4:10b). We spent some time in chapter 8 talking about the battle, that is, the struggle for our mind, specifically our peace of mind, and the battle for our hearts to serve temporal masters. Jabez knew this; we know this. As you pray, remind the enemy God has already won. He can be trusted. He is our protector.

> He who dwells in the shelter of the Most Hight will rest in the shadow of the Almighty. I will see of the Lord, "He is my refuge and my fortress, my God in whom I trust." … His faithfulness will be your shield and rampart. You will not fear the terror of night, nor the arrow that flies by day. (Psalm 91:1–2, 4b–6)

I continued to pray, asking God to give me a glimpse of this territory. In the following weeks, Brian and I attended a class taught by a pastor. This pastor had traveled the States for months, visiting from the Congo. It was his last evening in the United States. I knew nothing of him. I had no idea why he was here. Dear church friends had invited us to this class. They knew this pastor as an extremely learned man and invited him to speak to the leadership at our church. Two hours passed like two minutes. I felt we needed to give him something for the gift of his time and teaching. He had spoken so eloquently and with such passion. He had opened windows in my mind to spiritual warfare and the amazing power of the Holy Spirit. He told stories that made me want to be fierce like him. I was so grateful. I asked, "How can we pray for you?"

He went on to tell us about a school he had started in the Congo for marginalized children, children arriving at school hungry, many orphaned by at least one parent. These children were learning about Jesus by virtue of the call of this one man and His passion and prayer to enlarge His territory.

Since that time, we have not adopted but fallen in love with 350 Congolese children. We see videos of their singing, praying, and learning, and we are working to get them a well for water and provide more lunches. Our territory has been enlarged and enriched, and our hearts have been encouraged.

What is your Congo? Perhaps your territory lies beyond your current borders: the business you want to start, the ministry you wish to be a part of, or the book you want to write. All of the territories look different, but like the journey to fierce, He will provide the map, itinerary, and travel budget. He will show us how this is possible. His provision and our passion are a powerful combination. Lean into this, and He will confirm, create, and chart the course.

And what if you are already across the pond? What if your new ministry, work, or project has begun and it is not what you thought, the work seems too much, or the fulfillment too little? I have been there, and so was Elijah. Remember the story in 1 Kings 18, one of the greatest showdowns in history, Elijah versus 450 prophets of Baal. King Ahab and Queen Jezebel were running the country and dishonoring God in big, bad ways. The land of Samaria was in the midst of a terrible famine, lacking both food and water.

At high noon or thereabouts, they meet at Mt. Carmel. The 450 prophets built an altar to sacrifice to Baal, and Elijah likewise built an altar to sacrifice to God. Whoever's altar burned first would be declared winner. Elijah deferred to the 450 to call Baal down and start the fire on the altar. They yelled, sang, and pleaded, but there was not a spark. Elijah encouraged them to keep trying in the most sarcastic way, knowing God would be faithful.

Baal failed. Then Elijah, ready to call on God to start the fire on the altar, first turned to the servants and had them douse the altar with water, not once but three times. Water was pooling on and around the altar, and at that moment, God sent a fire, but not just any fire. The power of heaven came down, burning up the sacrifice, the stone, and even the water that had run off the altar. Moments later, Elijah ordered all the false prophets destroyed. As a *coup de grâce*, God then sent thunderous rain to cover the land.

I would think in the life of Elijah this was a very good day. But just moments later, as Jezebel heard of the defeat and embarrassment of her band of prophets, she called for the extermination of Elijah. He was scared and alone. He did exactly what you and I would do. He ran. But then the sweetest miracle occurred. God saw Elijah. He understood his fear. He answered his prayer and nourished his body.

> "I have had enough, LORD," he (Elijah) said. "Take my life; I am no better than my ancestors." Then he lay down under the bush and fell asleep. All at once an angel touched him and said, "Get up and eat." He looked around, and there by his head was some bread baked over hot coals, and a jar of water. He ate and drank and then lay down again. The angel of the LORD came back a second time and touched him and said, "Get up and eat, for the journey is too much for you." So he got up and ate and drank. Strengthened by that food, he traveled forty days and forty nights until he reached Horeb, the mountain of God. (1 Kings 19:4b–8)

Do you need that touch, encouragement, and nourishment? He knows, sees, hears, and answers prayer. He is not capricious; nor does He hide His hand, love, will, or provision from us. He makes His presence known in the answers to our prayers. "For the LORD God is our sun and our shield. He gives us grace and glory. The LORD will withhold no good thing from those who do what is right" (Psalm 84:11 NLT).

"He withholds no good thing"

He is in this for our good. We are in it for His glory. Pray for your territory to be enlarged. Pray to find Him in every corner of your life. Pray to unlock the doors of your heart to the freedom of faith and forgiveness. Pray the testimony of your life reveals the Redeemer. He is faithful, good, and true. He will never ever not answer when you earnestly seek Him. He makes the weak heart brave.

10

La Fin

We believers use phrases and scripture like candy in jars, extracting one or a handful as the time or circumstance sweetens the need. I have said and believed for as long as I can remember that this life is a journey, but I have rarely considered my path or purpose. Our path, our purpose, begins and ends with Him. The start of the journey is our birth into His family; it is the day, the moment, we called Him our Father.

I wonder when it was for you. Were you a child in Sunday school or an adult in church? Were you listening to a preacher or a persistent friend? Did you confess at the altar or in the still, small space of your mind? Did you feel the Holy Spirit rush in and embrace you as you laid your sins down and felt the weight of a ransom lifted off your soul? Did you give Him your life as a child and then took it back for the last five months or fifty years? Have you struggled to stay on the path?

This path, this journey, has a definite beginning in birth and an absolute end in death. The Word tells us, "His mercies are new every morning" (Lamentations 3:22–23). Yet we know He is the same yesterday, today, and forever. Why does He dust off His mercies on a daily basis? Where did you leave off last night? How did your day end? If you look at your path, were you ten steps ahead or forty-two back? We start where we finished the day before, but remember, there is glory, hope, and healing because all of us are still on the path. We are still walking in faith. We are still on the journey toward heaven. We may have stepped back. We call it "backslid" down home. But He is still the goal. We pick up, pray up, and pursue more of Him.

His capacity to forgive and His incomparable love does not diminish due to yesterday. The mercies are new, available, fresh, and free. Let's grab hold.

My thoughts as I leave you here, as I hope and pray that your fear is ebbing to fierce, I charge you with courage because that is the essence of the God we serve, one that would not have us in bondage to discouragement and fear but to hope and fearlessness. I pray the very same words Paul penned two thousand years ago that from the storehouse of

> His glorious riches He may strengthen you with power through His spirit in your inner being so that Christ may dwell in your hearts through faith. And I pray that you, being rooted and established in love, may have power, together with all the saints, to grasp how wide and long and high and deep is the love of Christ, and to know this love that surpasses knowledge—that you may be **FILLED TO THE MEASURE WITH THE FULLNESS OF GOD.** Now to Him who is able to do immeasurably more than all we ask or imagine, according to His power that is at work within us, to Him be glory in the church and in Christ Jesus throughout all generations, forever and ever. Amen. (Ephesians 3:16–21, emphasis added)

Dear one, stand firm on your **F**oundation and walk. Hold His hand and **I**nvite Him in. **E**xperience His presence. **R**ejoice with Him as He rejoices over you. Embrace your **C**all knowing you and I are here to know Him and let Him be known by others. And finally **E**nlarge your territory. Fill the spaces of your soul with the confidence that being fierce is within your grasp and fear no longer has its grip.

- **F**—Foundation (knowing who we are in Christ)
- **I**—Inviting Jesus into every corner of our lives
- **E**—Experiencing His presence
- **R**—Rejoice (embracing joy at all times in all circumstances)
- **C**—Calling (knowing what He has made us for)
- **E**—Enlarging our territory

It has been my absolute joy to write these words and share them with you. **Go in joy, FIERCE warrior. I love you so.**

Fierce Footsteps—Steps to Help You on Your Journey

1. Foundation

Take a psalm and begin to write out God's promises. The living Word of God and living Spirit within you will be faithful to point out the promises. It will be the promises you need today and the ones you will need next week.

Begin with Psalm: _____

My promises from God to me are:

_____

_____

_____

_____

2. Invitation

Perhaps you resonated with a negative emotion. Maybe you know the exact moment where this feeling began. Or possibly, like me, you are not sure where it started, but you would love to make this hot, crusted emotion a warm ally. What is the emotion?

_____

Find a quiet space and a bit of time. Ask Him to sit with you and identify this emotion. I guarantee He will not be surprised, disappointed, mad, or unforgiving. He will sit in this space and reveal how crazy in love He is with this part of you. He wants to lead you out of the alone part of this. Take a moment to write to Him about it. The act of writing is an act of surrender. It is a declaration that He can come into this place. He can be a part of this pain and lead you through the door of healing.

_____

_____

_____

_____

3. Experience His Presence

Reflect on where and when you can meet God. Pick one of the following and dedicate this next week to finding Him here.

I will meet Him

- During this mundane task _____.
- During this time of day _____.
- When I read my Bible, I will pull up a chair and acknowledge He is there with me.
- When I see people at work, school, neighborhood, or shopping, I will whisper His name.
- When I speak to people, I will silently pray for them.

- I will hum this song or hymn throughout the day because it reminds me that He is here.
- As I rise in the morning, I will give Him my entire day.

4. Rejoicing

Rejoicing can be found in two distinct practices: surrender and prayer. Write down what is troubling you, which seems to be stealing your joy.

_____

In writing this down, surrender it to Him. Approach Him with the confidence that He is working even this thing for your good. As you give this thing to Him in prayer, commit to leaving it with Him and then look for Him. Take a walk or look out your window. Remove the lens of this current trouble and ask to see Him. If you are sitting in the dark or walking is not an option, open to the psalms. Let Him speak His promises to you, but do not stop there. Rejoice in the covering of His care. Do not let the shadow of this current trouble extinguish the light. Rather let the light shower the trouble. Watch it grow smaller as His hand holds you and it. Rejoice not in the removal of the hurt or pain, but in the presence of the Healer.

5. Calling

What are you passionate about?

_____

What did you dream about doing?

_____

When you were very young, before ten years old?

_____

As a teen?

_____

In college or after high school?

_____

What do you fear the most?

_____

What would you do if you had three months to live?

_____

What would you do if money was no object?

_____

6. Enlarging our Territory

This the last step, and you might find it is the easiest because, dear traveler, this is not our work, but His. Commit to these words, and this prayer of Jabez for the days and weeks to come and watch Him work. Pray for eyes to see and ears to hear as He shows you your role as a fierce warrior for Him. Pray this, "God bless me. God enlarge my territory. God keep me from harm and pain."

Watch as your thoughts turn from work to worship. Listen as your have-tos become get-tos. And pray that your wild hope becomes action. He is faithful.

Write down the territory He is mapping in your mind. Let no possibility be off limits. Let the Creator create and let you, His creations, be FIERCE.

_____

_____

_____

_____

Works Cited

Buechner, Frederick. *Wishful Thinking*. New York: Harper Collins, 1993.

Giglio, Louie. "Never Cease to Pray." Passion Conference, Passion Church, October 8, 2019, Atlanta, GA.

Goff, Bob. "A Flood of Love." Rocky Mount Events Center, September 13, 2019, Rocky Mount, NC.

"How Do You Define Joy?" https://www.desiringgod.org/articles/how-do-you-define-joy.

Laubach, Frank Charles. *The Game with Minutes: Practicing the Presence of God*. London: 1959.

Lenzkes, Susan. *Women's Devotional Bible 2, with Psalms and Proverbs*. Grand Rapids, Mich.: Zondervan Publishing, 1999.

Lewis, C. S. *The Weight of Glory*. San Francisco: Harper One, 2001.

———. *Mere Christianity*. New York: Harper Collins, 2001.

———. *The Screwtape Letters*. San Francisco: Harper One, 2015.

Maslow, Abraham H. *Theory of Human Motivation*. Wilder Publications, 2018.

"Walter Cannon: Stress & Fight or Flight Theories." study.com/academy/lesson/walter-cannon-stress-fight-or-flight-theories.html.

Wiersby, Walter. *Be Determined*. Colorado Springs: David Cook, 1992.

Further Reading

Cook, Alllison, and Kimberly Miller. *Boundaries for Your Soul*. Nashville: Thomas Nelson, 2018.

Lewis, C. S. *Mere Christianity*. New York: Harper Collins, 2001.

CPSIA information can be obtained
at www.ICGtesting.com
Printed in the USA
LVHW111354140321
681507LV00022B/139